THE UGLY SIDE OF AMERICA

A Society that Still Devalues Black Males!

By

Minister Bryant Keith Williams Sr.

ISBN-13: 978-1500127312
ISBN-10: 1500127310

"The future of the black race lies within the young black male"

-Tupac Amaru Shakur-

(June 16, 1971– September 13, 1996

CONTENTS

About the Author

Minister Bryant Keith Williams is a California native, the youngest of eleven siblings and has been married to his wife, Marguerite, for twenty-two years. He have three sons ages 17, 19, and 21. He earned his AA Degree at South West Bible College in Moreno Valley, CA and a BA in Religion and Leadership in Ministry at Vanguard University in Costa Mesa, CA. He is currently working on his MA Education Counseling and Clinical Psychology degree at Azusa Pacific University in Azusa, CA. He is also an ordained minister; he spent several years working as a licensed Cabinet and Millworks Contractor; he started his own non-profit ministry, *Safe Haven,* several years ago.

Min. Bryant Keith Williams is also an emerging screenwriter with several scripts under his belt. His script, *Rightful Place*, is a positive story about an African American pastor who volunteers in a *Clergy on Campus* program at a middle school. In that role, he prevents a school shooting which could have been a massacre. In his second script, *Something Has to Die*, the story is based on racism and mental health issues. The major character is an African American ex-cop by the name of Christopher Dorner who went on a shooting rampage after being fired from the LAPD. Minister Williams is currently working on another script called *Unnecessary Hate*; it is a story that combines the Trayvon Benjamin Martin's and Jordan Davis' homicides. The storyline is plagued with issues of racism and injustice.

Introduction

When I was seventeen, I joined my brother in committing a crime. I was the lookout while he stripped a set of rims off an abandoned vehicle in my old neighborhood, in Los Angeles, California. Just before he could approach the vehicle and remove the rims, a police cruiser hit the corner and chirped the siren. We took off running! I was a pretty fast runner back then and I cleared the fences like hurdles on a track field.

I ran into a backyard and was suddenly boxed in with nowhere to hide, except for an old vehicle. I crawled beneath it, and I was so afraid I began to pray, "God, please, if you get me out of this I will never commit another crime in my young, black life ever again." There was more to my prayer but an officer snatched me from under the vehicle proceeded to stomp and pummel me. I was choked and I even blacked out for a few seconds. As the white cop choked me, his face was full of rage, as if I assaulted someone in his family.

The police brutality was typical, that is the Modus Operandi of most racist cops. But it was not justifiable. The officer put his weapon to my head and asked, "Who was that with you? Why did you run?"

"I don't know him," I said. "I just met him."

"You're lying," he responded. "I'm going to blow your fucking head off." He pressed the gun hard against my temple. "You're dead, nigger."

I thought he was going to shoot me so I broke down and spewed out "It was my brother." The cop asked where I lived, then he drove me to my father's house around the corner.

I sat in the backseat of the squad car as the cops went inside my father's house They disrespected and roughed up my dad and oldest brother, destroyed property, and apprehended my brother for running. Both of my brothers bore physical scars from the police brutality. The cops actually high-fived each other, as if capturing a slave master's runaways.

On the way to the precinct, I prayed for something out of the ordinary to happen to the squad car – a freak accident, like the vehicle flipping over and killing everyone but my brother and me. I accept the boneheaded decision I made that day, but did the malicious behavior of the cops fit the crime? Did the cop have to use racial epithets towards me? They didn't have to assault my dad and oldest brother, as well as destroy our property. However, they did what white racist males in power have done for centuries, and that is wield their authority in a racist and reckless manner by any means necessary .

In this book, I will be focusing on racially motivated incidents, the pattern of historical and existential racism, the criminality and fatalities that manifest at the hands of white law enforcement agents, as well as southern white males across the nation. This type of devaluing not only hinges on historical hatred, but it is the worst kind of mandate since the COINTELPRO Operation, which was designed to target and eliminate allegedly radical individuals and groups in America, instituted by the FBI under J. Edgar Hoover's leadership. Nonetheless, I will include *Action- step(s)* at the end of each chapter, salient solutions at the end of the book, as well as a discussion page.

CHAPTER ONE

Still Open Season On Black Males

"Being a black man in America isn't easy...the hunt is on and you're the prey"

-Charles Dutton-

The above quote is from the Hughes Brothers' movie, *Menace II Society,* a provocative film that depicts the real issues black males face across the nation, specifically black-on-black crime. In non-racially motivated incidents, a black male has a higher percentage of being killed by another black man than someone of the white majority culture. However, Black men need to understand the psychology behind the historical and existential devaluing they face, and how systematic racism is perpetuated against black males more than any other culture of men. I believe that awareness, anger, and action is needed- like never before because of the pervasive criminality, mass incarceration, and unacceptable murdering of countless Black males across America. It's a shame that a Black male still has to look both ways when leaving his home and worry about being targeted by white law enforcement agents or some gun toting southern racist as well as someone of his own culture. However, the quote by Charles Dutton above-mentioned should serve as a reality check for every Black male in America. The fact is black on black crime contributes to the "Purge" that is underway in society in regards to the annihilation of black males. The sad reality is, far too many black males are like Deer's on the road at night, finding themselves facing head lights and death because of no sense of history or hope.

Historically, white hatred towards blacks has been passed down from generation to generation. Southern lynch parties were considered legalized hunting on black males, and looking back at the past of such sinister acts, one can understand the current behavior of the generation of racism towards black males. After all, our lives meant nothing to whites back then, and it seems that sentiment continues today.

Let us focus on three psychology terms: *empathy*, *antipathy,* and *reaction aggression. Empathy* is the ability to understand the emotions and concerns of another person, especially when they differ from one's own. *Antipathy* is feelings of dislike or even hatred for another person. *Reaction aggression* is an impulsive retaliation for another person's intentional or accidental action, verbal or physical (Berger, 2011). Now, which term do you think America has displayed towards black males? I can tell you from experience that black males haven't witnessed much societal, socioeconomic or judicial *empathy* from their white counterparts.

I've learned by raising kids that if you treat a child with antipathy and tell a child repeatedly, "You're nothing; you're worthless; just kill yourself," how do you think that child will respond? Most children project their abuse, becoming a threat to themselves or others. And that is just what systematic America has done in regards to the black male. She has told the black male socioeconomically and judicially, "You're a criminal, a thug; you can't be trusted; you're subhuman, worthless, and your life doesn't mean anything to us." Black males have been conditioned with this negative reinforcement, so long as black-on-black crime makes sense to a *"reactive aggressive"* culture.

Nonetheless, *antipathy* has been shown towards black males at the hand of white law enforcement agents to destroy the black male without any *empathy* and consequences. The question is, what have black males done to be treated so abnormally? It seems that America has displayed antipathy toward black males through mass incarceration and unarmed shootings, and the "industrial prison complex," a haven for honing criminality, has done the most damage. According to Michelle Alexander, Author of the New Jim Crow "The system of mass incarceration now seems normal and natural to most, a regrettable necessity" (Alexander, 2010-2012). Mrs. Alexander touches on the acceptance of such treatment towards a whole generation of men and women. It is shameful how America kicks her feet up, and enjoys the fruit of the labor from mass incarceration at the expense of so many minorities. The judicial system makes it a priority to lock up as many black males as possible, more than their white counter parts because racist prosecutors and judges believe prison is some kind of normal habitat for black males. However, let us examine a real American horror story in regards to the lynching of Jesse Washington.

Historical Lynching:

The historical hatred of black men is incredulous and unforgivable, and the Jim Crow South has been a killing field in regards to black males. For instance, an African American Southerner by the name of Jesse Washington was tortured and burned alive in May 1916 in Waco, Texas. According to Ehrenhaus (2004), as many as 15,000 men, women, and children congregated to observe and participate in the lynching. What is so incredulous about this incident is Mr. Washington was a mentally retarded teenager. The jury deliberated four minutes before finding him guilty. A guilty verdict was just the beginning of Mr. Washington's woe. A white mob dragged him from the courtroom, bound him in chains, ripped off his clothes and cut them into souvenir pieces. The mob went as far too cut his ear off and unsexed him" (Ehrenhaus, 2004, pp. 286-287). There are cases like this that make the hair stand up on the back of my neck; however, this was the type of terrorism that many African American men had to endure. The fact that some could resort to such behavior without conviction proves that racism was legal and enforced in the South. This was definitely a horrific act, and I wonder what was going through Mr. Washington's mind during the torture?

I believe the citizens of this particular town decided to play judge, jury, and executioner. They deliberated for only "four minutes." Wow, it seems they had no intention of giving Mr. Washington the benefit of being proven innocent before guilty. They cared less about his mental disability. The question is where were the lawmen of this day? I'll tell you where; they were right there partaking in the terrorist act against this black male with a disability. They didn't see a human being or a mentally challenged and probably innocent male. No. To these savages, Mr. Washington was a threat, a nigger, and a coon; he was also inferior being that he allegedly raped one of their prize possessions (a white female).

This is why some people don't want have anything to do with Christianity because of the demonic behavior of whites claiming to be Christian. Most conservative westerners have the audacity to make allegations about Islamic terrorists, but the first act, of terrorism and devaluing of black males was conducted by so-called white extreme Christians. The author sheds light on Protestant Christians and their ritualistic ideology associated with sacrificial lynching's.

> Brutal and barbaric features of sacrificial lynching, torture and mutilation; burning and incineration; the collection of body fragments and the purchase and circulation of photographs as sacred relics—were constitutive acts of the perpetrators' Christian faith (Ehrenhaus, 2004, p. 2)

Wow. Acts of "sacrificial lynching, torture, mutilation, burning and incineration "was some form of worship. This is why, some have called the white- race, "Blue-eyed-devils." How could one culture devalue another for simply the color of one's skin? Most of all, how could a culture use The Bible as justification to devalue and destroy another human being/culture for sick reasons? I believe this historical behavior is quite demonic in nature.

Ehrenhaus (2004) continues:

> The post-Reconstruction era of Jim Crow, the ritual performance of mass mob, sacrificial lynching functioned for the dominant white Christian community as acts of devotion and defense, as blood sacrifices to a God whose covenant with the white Christian community had been violated by the intrusion of blackness into the sacred spaces of that covenant (p.2).

This is astounding, that a culture would justify eliminating another and hinge that behavior and belief on some type of decree by the Creator of the universe. The Creator of the universe never sanctioned a ritual of mass extermination, lynching, and blood sacrifice of black males. Unfortunately, this belief has been engrained in the thinking of some in the majority culture; especially, those in positions of power positions-like law enforcement, judicial, religious and educational institutions. This is why sacrificing Mr. Washington like he was a burnt offering seemed normal to them. To make matters worse, these were religious folks, individuals who used the Holy Bible and twisted it to suit their own savagery toward blacks. There is an authority-figure on race issues in America by the name of Apostle Fredrick K.C. Price and the author of *Race Religion & Racism*. He exposed the mindset of a so-called white Bible scholar, Chares Carroll.

Carroll's statement is as follows:

> The white is the highest and the Negro the lowest, of the so-called five races of men; and they present the most striking contrast to each other in their physical and mental char-

acters, their modes of life, habits, customs, manners, language, gestures, etc (Price, 2001).

It's individuals like Mr. Carroll and others that have perpetuated negative notions about blacks being inferior and unintelligent. One may say, "This is just an individual blowing off some steam; however, the last time someone blew off some verbal steam six million Jews were exterminated and millions of African slaves were displaced, devalued and destroyed. Mr. Carroll and other white men have circulated material like *The Tempter of Eve*, and this type of rhetoric has permeated the minds of white law enforcement agents, judges, prosecutors, businessman, and educators whom have decided the fate of so many minorities, through, racial profiling, stop and frisk, police brutality, judicial lynching, mass incarceration, denial of college admission and employment. Today, Black males may not face a similar public lynching like Mr. Jesse Washington, but the number of racially motivated killings of black males prove that it is still "open season" on black males. Nonetheless, let's take a look at most recent incidents. I believe we'll start to see a pattern crystallize.

Unjustifiable Targeting:

There's been a wave of unjustifiable and unacceptable police shootings of black males in the past five-years as well as white-male citizens hiding behind the so-called "Stand your ground" law in many southern states. Before I address this issue, let's reflect on the following names:

Trayvon Martin (17), Jordan Davis (17), Kendrec McCade (19), Kimari Grey (17), Timothy Russell and passenger Malissa Williams was killed- cop fired 137 rounds, Ervin Jefferson (18), Amadou Diallo (23), Patrick Dorismond (26), Ousman Zongo (43), Timothy Stansbury Jr. (19) Sean

Bell (23), Orlando Barlow (28), Aaron Campbell (25), Victor Steen (17), Steven Eugene Washington (27), Alonzo Ahsley (29), Wendell Allen (20), Ronald Madison (40) & James Brisette (17), Traveres MeGill (16), Remarley Graham (18), Oscar Grant (22), *Dane Scott Jr. (17).*

I wish I could address each case, but there are just too many; however, I will focus on some incidents that have gained national attention. The million dollar question is, "Why are so many young black males still being targeted in a post- racial society"? Some may respond, "Well, black males are committing the most crimes." This is a typical response, but understandable because there is so much 'black on black crime.'

The abovementioned names of unarmed black males killed by white law enforcement agents and white male citizens validates the disdain America exhibits towards minorities. The refuting fact is, unarmed black males are being racially profiled and killed at an alarming rate. Sadly, we as a nation have normalized the killings by being passive and poised about the issue. The unjustifiable murdering of African American males are happening far too often, and they're being targeted because they simply look suspicious or are wearing clothing which some associate with criminality. No individual should be gunned down by someone who is supposed to protect and serve their citizens. This is the current dilemma in black America. The fact is that black boys are not coming home due to racial profiling and a paranoid society which believes they are a threat. The number of black males racially murdered or incarcerated (1 in 3) should serve as a "wakeup call" for every African American parent.

As a parent, I have three sons and since the killing of so many of our African American boys, I've been on edge. I believe a lot of parents in the African American community suffer from this type of phobia as well. We pray that our children will be judged by the content of their character, but instead they're being gunned down because of the color of their skin. The Trayvon Martin Trial remind us that we live in a society that is no different from the Jim Crow South. We live in a society that suggests that it's okay to murder a black male because at the end of the day, they're just sub human.

Moreover, I believe there's commonality in the killings of black males versus the Jim Crow South. First and foremost, each one of these black males listed in this chapter were killed by a white male and most were lawmen. In the Jim Crow South, the Klan (white males) drove around at night and captured black males who have been either allegedly accused of killing, whistling, looking or speaking to a white woman or they were just out to kill a black male for sport. To solidify my point, Emmett Louis Till (July 25, 1941–August 28, 1955) was an African-American boy who was murdered in Mississippi at the age of 14 after reportedly flirting with a white woman. Till was from Chicago, Illinois, visiting his relatives in Mississippi, when he allegedly whistled at the 21-year-old Carolyn Bryant, the married proprietor of a small grocery store there. Bryant's husband Roy and his half-brother J. W. Milam arrived at Till's great-uncle's house where they took Till, transported him to a barn, beat him and gouged out one of his eyes, before shooting him through the head. His body was discovered and retrieved from the river three days later (Samuels, 2013).

Emmett Till was maimed and murdered beyond human recognition just for allegedly whistling or speaking to a white women. Oprah Winfrey caught flack by comparing the Trayvon Martin case to the Emmett Till murder. Her assessment of the two cases was not well received by conservatives who refuted her claims. Oprah was referring to the racial pattern of these types of killings, not the style of such killings. The fact is the killings are racial, unjustifiable and normalized. The style by which black males are killed may have changed, but the intent remains. The fact is, in the South high ranking officials were either involved or supported lynching's. According to WalDrep (2008), he shares some astounding information in his article and how the Department of Justice (DOJ) abruptly reversed itself and sent agents of the Federal Bureau of Investigation (FBI) into the South to investigate reported lynching's.

WalDrep (2008):

> Some of the most elite legal scholars writing at the height of the lynching era agreed that poorly performing courts promoted lynching. The people considered themselves a law unto themselves. Since they make the laws judges must follow, they can take over the function of a judge (pp. 595-596).

The white judges and prosecutors didn't care about the fate of black men because they were probably the ones holding the rope and cans of gasoline as the lynching's were conducted. Southern lynching's was a community effort, and black males didn't stand a chance in that type of hostile culture. Today, it seems we still don't stand a chance in a dominant culture where unjustifiable unarmed shootings of black males is becoming the norm. There was a particular case that got national attention and the court's ruling sent a shock wave of disbelief across the nation.

Predatory killing:

An African American male by the name of Trayvon Benjamin Martin (age 17) was unjustifiable targeted and murdered; on February 26, 2012. Mr. Martin walked from a Sanford, Florida convenient store with a pack of Skittles and a can of Arizona tea in his Hoodie sweater just to be unjustifiable murdered (shot) by George Zimmerman. Mr. Zimmerman was a white Hispanic neighborhood watch volunteer. Mr. Zimmerman appeared on the conservative Fox News (Sean Hannity); he gave a candid and casual response about the night he shot an unarmed Trayvon Martin. The interview was unfortunate because Mr. Zimmerman could've cleared any doubts about his reasons for firing a fatal shot to Mr. Martin's chest. However, he made a senseless statement as to why, he believe Mr. Martin deserved to die on that fateful night in a Sanford, Florida housing complex.

Hannity asked Zimmerman if he had any regrets if, for example, he wished he hadn't gotten out of the car or if he would have done anything differently. Mr. Zimmerman answered, "No sir." He continued, saying, "I feel that it was all God's plan and for me to second guess it or judge it…" *(Friedman, 2013)*.

Mr. Zimmerman's adamant, "No sir" and belief that killing an unarmed, seventeen-year- old black male was part of "God's plan" is quite sinister. I believe Mr. Zimmerman's fear the night of the shooting was racially motivated. I believe Mr. Zimmerman had to be taught to dislike young black males. It is clear that race played a role in this particular shooting based on the negative overtones shared by the shooter. Mr. Zimmerman seemed comfortable in his own skin when killing Trayvon Benjamin Martin.

Min. Louis Farrakhan, a great social voice, said, "In retaliation for President Barack Obama's election, it will be dangerous for black people!" This assessment is true because white cops, militias, and others have been gearing up for possibilities of a race war across America.

According to a CNN report:

> Racist anger toward Obama was evident even before he became president. Two weeks before Obama won, authorities said they foiled a skinhead plot to assassinate him. The two suspects, based in Tennessee, also apparently planned to shoot and decapitate dozens of African-Americans, the Bureau of Alcohol, Tobacco, Firearms and Explosives said (Chen, 2013).

The wave of unarmed killings of black males, unjustifiable

homicides, Stand Your Ground cases, and hate crimes have developed since president Barack Obama's election. Yes, white college kids were also instrumental in President Obama's election; however, white college kids are not the initial problem, but it's the angry, extremist, Southern conservative (white) racist in power positions (where it matters the most). Unfortunately, they end up encouraging the younger generation of whites like Adolph Hitler did in Nazi Germany through dogma, rhetoric, doctrine, and hate speech. I believe the miseducating about black males continues in America. This is why, so much hatred has been targeted against black males and why inherited hatred flourishes because some racist dads or granddads bestow disdain for the black male upon their sons. This is why Mr. Zimmerman was so comfortable with predatorily killing an unarmed, seventeen year old, Trayvon Benjamin Martin on February 26, 2012.

Color-coded cowards on the loose:

The next case is appalling: an African American, eight- year-old Donald Maiden Jr. was not killed, but the scar of the incident would forever hunt him. The development of this case is so incredulous that after reading it, I see why the phrase "Justice for all" is simply just a catch phrase instead of a reality for most in black America.

Brian Cloninger, a 46 year old white male, shot an 8-year-old African American child, Donald Maiden Jr., in the face, and has been granted reduced bail. Cloninger's attorney asked that the amount be reduced by lowering the bail from $2.2 million to $1 million, even though this was not as low as Cloninger wanted. Investigators believe Cloninger, who had a serious problem with alcoholism was drinking when he decided to shoot the child in the face at the boy's Lake Highlands apartment complex. One witness approached Cloninger after the shooting and has stated to police that the shooter admitted, **"Yeah, I shot that kid."** When the witnessed asked why, Cloninger said, "**Because I wanted to**." (Wooten, 2013).

Some may ask, "What did an eight- year old child do to be shot in the face"? This grown man decided to go outside his home... aim a pistol at an innocent eight-year old child and pull the trigger. This is unfathomable hate and based on the reduction in bail for Mr. Cloninger, the system sends a negative message about justice. It appears that the system did not care about prosecuting Mr. Cloninger to the full extent of the law for his actions. This so-called "blame it on the alcohol" excuse is no different from Flip Wilson's famous line that says, "The devil made me do it". Mr. Cloninger displayed behavior that has been waged against black males for so long in this country. Mr. Cloninger said, "**I shot that kid because I wanted to**". His casual response is most appalling and inexcusable; the court had the audacity to reduce his bail. We see a cognitive connection between Mr. Cloninger and Mr. Zimmerman which shows commonality in such shootings of unarmed black males. The casual responses of these gentlemen, during the killing of black males is totally unacceptable.

Lastly, I want to share a very disturbing admission via letter of a very disingenuous and recalcitrant racist, Michael Dunn, the Florida man charged with shooting seventeen-year old Jordan Davis after an argument over loud Hip Hop music. In this letter, you will see Mr. Dunn's true intentions about his feelings or phobia about black males, in particular Hip hop artists. The letter is lengthy so I will only focus on key aspects.

In a letter to his grandmother Mr. Dunn's rants from incarceration:

> The jail is full of blacks and they all act like thugs. This may sound a bit radical, but if more people would arm themselves and kill these (expletive) idiots, when they're threatening you, eventually they may take the hint and change their behavior. I'm really not prejudiced against race, but I have no use for certain cultures. This gangster-

rap, ghetto talking thug 'culture' that certain segments of society flock to is intolerable. They espouse violence and disrespect towards women (Cadet, 2013).

If we dissect the letter, we can most likely come up with a logical conclusion as to why, Mr. Dunn not only shot seventeen year old Jordan Davis, but the ecology behind his hatred for being a color-coded, racist bigot. The letter to his grandma is proof that the killing of a black male with little remorse exposes his upbringing. I am willing to bet that Dunn's father, grandfather, or uncle passed down racial hatred in regard to black males being "thugs."

In the first paragraph, Mr. Dunn says, "The jail is full of blacks and they all act like thugs." This is exactly how racist white males in power positions, such as law enforcement, prosecutors, and most conservatives, think about black males. They feel that black males are thugs, and Hoodie wearing criminals. This is all white code-language for depicting and devaluing a whole culture of individuals unloved by the majority in this country. Besides, Mr. Dunn's radical solution for the black "thug" problem suggests that "more people to arm themselves and kill these idiots"; this shows his racial intent; when he shot a seventeen year old, Jordan Davis three- times. The investigation yielded that Jordan Davis and three occupants were not armed, but Jordan Davis was killed for simply not turning down the "loud music". Finally, Mr. Dunn became political in his letter and blamed "liberal media" for too much attention to his case. He had wanted an all white jury because he said, "My fear is that if I get one black person on my jury, it will be a mistrial as I am convinced they will be racially biased." Well, he was right about a mistrial, "A jury in Jacksonville found Michael Dunn guilty of attempted second-degree murder for opening fire on three other teens in the same SUV as Jordan Davis but deadlocked on the murder charge against him in Davis' death" (Botelho, 2014). Mr. Dunn claims he's not a racist, but his language, context, and euphuisms' suggests otherwise.

Action steps:

1. Young black males must stop giving law enforcement agents a reason to squeeze the trigger.
2. I believe if many black males exhibit good manners in society instead of reacting negatively towards law enforcement agents some situations would be defused.
3. To alleviate the chronic issue of police brutality and fatalities of black males, law enforcement agents need more than just sensitivity training but cultural competency training; they should have one- hour every week of personal or group therapy to help them express and alleviate some of their bias and frustrations that come along with working in urban areas.

Nonetheless, the bottom line is, black males are in trouble; not only because of black-on-black crime and defamation of our own women, but because of a nonchalant nation that does not care much about what happens to them. Lawmakers refuse to implement real solutions to preserve and value the black males in America. There appears to be more value placed on males of other cultures including White, Asian and alternatively Hispanic because they appear to be less threatening and more profitable. This brings me to the next chapter, in which I will address America's fear and austere behavior towards black males. Most of all, I will examine the prevailing reasons why I believe that black males are treated as a "National Threat."

CHAPTER TWO

National Threat!

In 1968, just two years after Oakland residents, Huey Newton and Bobby Seale, formed the Black Panthers, FBI Director J Edgar Hoover called the party "the greatest threat to the internal security of the country".

-(Manus, 2010)-

As a nation, we have militaristically managed to neutralize foreign threats of terrorism, but on the other hand, we have failed to address systematic terrorism in our own front yard. According to Alexander, (2010) "It seems that criminalization and demonization of black men is one habit America seems unlikely to break" *(Alexander, 2010-2012)*. The statement, "Criminalization and demonization is a habit America is unlikely to break" is the basis for maladaptive behavior of white law enforcement agents and gun wielding racists towards black males. I believe J. Edgar Hoover's statement about the Black Panther Party (BPP) being a "the greatest threat to the internal security of the country" is euphemistically stated. It is important for everyone to become knowledgeable about the 1960s and the upheaval that existed; this was a pivotal time for the Civil Rights' movement. The assumption of Mr. Hoover about the (BPP) "being a "threat" may not seem like a negative assessment to some; but it was his private thought towards this particular group of black men, which gave credence to his public actions of waging war on the (BPP). Mr. Hoover ordered the incarceration and extermination of a culture of black men standing in their "rightful place" and fighting for a worthy cause. Based on the statement that the BPP is "the greatest threat to the internal security of the country" is Mr. Hoover's way of saying, blacks are the greatest threat to the internal security of white power. This is why, young black males need to understand that having "mo' money" isn't a restriction from being placed on Americas threat or watch-list. As African Americans, we need to wake up because with all of the mass incarceration and unarmed shootings, there seems to be a plot underway to rid this country of as many black males as possible. We must fight back by educating ourselves and educating our children how to live in such a diminishing society where they seem to be undervalued in so many ways.

Furthermore, if I had to diagnose America the case file would conclude that the system appears to be suffering from a Obsessive Compulsive Disorder of Mass Incarceration (OCDOMI). I believe this prognosis is dangerous and must be treated with aggressive activism. I believe America has a fetish for criminalizing black males and an obsession with the industrial prison complex of human warehousing. The fact is 60% of people in prison are now racial and ethnic minorities. The sad reality is Black males in their thirties, 1 in every 10 is in prison or jail on any given day (Racial Disparity, 2013). In comparison to whites, black males have a 1:3 ratio juxtapose to their white counterparts with a 1:17 ratio. Based on the statistics, black males are labeled as a national threat; therefore, they face social terrorism like stop and frisk, racial profiling, unjustifiable unarmed shootings and over prosecutorial practices. Nonetheless, there seems to be a much more sinister reason for America's phobia of the black male, which can be summed up in this phrase, "fear and fantasy." I will address the historical aspects of "fear and fantasy" as well as include some existential realities further.

Fear and fantasy:

First and foremost, Mandingo, a 1975 classic film, based on the novel *Mandingo* by *Kyle Onstott* and upon the play based thereon by *Jack Kirkland (Wikipedia, 2013)*. The film takes place on a run-down plantation owned by the widower Warren Maxwell

(*James Mason*) and his son Hammond (*Perry King*), a *Mandingo* slave Ganymede, or Mede (*Ken Norton*), is trained to fight other slaves. Hammond sexually neglects his wife Blanche (*Susan George*), discovering she was not a virgin. He rapes his black female slave Ellen (*Brenda Sykes*). However, his wife (Blanche) forces a balk male slave (Mede) to lay with her. The conflicting infidelities all eventually come together causing the film to end tragically.

The movie is significant because it speaks volumes about the plantation environment for black male and female slaves, but it also allows one to observe the psychological and emotional state of white slave masters and their wives. Yes, white slave masters and their wives and daughters suffered from "fear and fantasy". While white salve masters would violate black female slaves sexually, their wives and daughters had fantasies of their own about black male slaves. It is clear that the article supports my claims about 'fear and fantasy. According to an article by Foster (2011), there seem to have been a sexual fetish with white women fulfilling their sexual fantasies with Mulatto slaves. The fact is revenge sex with a black male slave (Mulattoe) was some type of leverage white women used against their horny husbands who were sleeping with black female slaves. Historically, we know white slave masters raped black female slaves, to not only fulfill their sick fantasy, but to break the spirit of the black male slave. After all, this is how Mulattoes, lighter skinned blacks were created as well. Some wives of slave masters got back at their cheating husbands by demanding sexual services from black male slaves (Mulattoes).

The author says:

> It was an extremely common thing among all the handsome mulattoes at the South to have connection with the white women. In this patriarchal society the sexual abuse of "nearly white" men could enable white women to enact

radical fantasies of domination over white men with the knowledge that their victim's body was legally black and enslaved, subject to the women's control. Although we have no evidence for a sexual fetish market in black male flesh, historical scholarship shows us that black male bodies might well be eroticized by white observers. Anglo-American culture long held a fascination with the penises of black men and projected both desire and jealousy upon an objectified and disembodied black phallus (Foster, 2011).

Wow, the black male was not only a slave, but an object of desire by white women on plantations. The fact that the author mentions "we have no record of such market" doesn't suggests that this is a myth. We have no record of a lot of historical facts, but that doesn't mean it's untrue. After all, I don't think whites want this ugly secret as a part of history. This would paint a bad picture of the western culture, and America doesn't want any negative depictions of their history. Based on the history books, there appears to be clear acknowledgement of great achievements of this nation and less about the short- comings we have endured. The fact is that white women chose Mulattoes to fulfill their fantasies because this type of male slave had some white blood in their DNA. However, according to the "one drop blood theory," which is a historical colloquial term in the United States for the social classification as Negro of individuals with any African ancestry, meaning any person with "one drop of Negro blood" was considered black" (Wikipedia, 2013). The author mentions something that is key, he says, "Anglo-American culture long held a fascination with the penises of black men and projected both desire and jealousy upon an objectified and disembodied black phallus" (Foster, 2011).

This is where the initial fear comes in at. In the movie *Mandingo,* we see the inferiority displayed by the white slave master or what the author calls, "Desire and jealousy upon an objectified and disembodied black phallus" (Foster , 2011). Yes, "desire and jealousy", these two-terms are sibling terms to the idea of "fear and fantasy" as well.

In America today, I believe this is why there have been historical killings like the (Emit Louis Till, Aug. 28 1955); Mr. Till was accused of flirting with a white women by the name of Carolyn Bryant. This was absurd that a fourteen year old boy would be flirting with a twenty-one year old white woman.

The racism towards black males may be a historical issue, but its evolution presents challenges for the twenty-first century. There are still phobias that exist in our so-called post racial society. White women have been forbidden from the black male, but so many of them are fulfilling their fantasies; some have even been ostracized and disowned by their families. For example, during my graduate program, I took a course where classmates had to present a cultural Genogram in a class of about forty- five students. One particular white female student shared during her presentation, a strict warning from her grandma. The grandmother said, "If you ever date outside of your race, in particularly a black man, I will disowned you."

In addition, one day I was caching up on a college assignment at Panera Bread Restaurant. Two elderly white females sat down and began sharing their Christian faith amongst themselves. I was impressed with their stance in sharing their faith unapologetically in a public setting. However, the conversation took a turn as one of the elderly females began to share her thoughts on interracial marriage. She said," I'm Christian, but I would like for my children to marry within their own culture because there's just too many problems that's attached to such unions (interracial)." Wow, I said to myself... "Shut the front door twice!" The second female was not in cahoots; she responded, "If two people (male and female) are truly in love and they're equally yoked, I don't see anything wrong with interracial marriages." I said to myself, "Good response sister; kudos too you!" Unfortunately , the first female stuck by her view and gave a lame reason as to why she's for same- race relationships.

I share this story because this supports my female classmates situation in regards to her grandma saying that she'd "Disown her if she married out of her race," in particular to a black man. How dare an individual claim to be a Christ follower, but don a 'white marrying white only' belief system as well. The apostle Paul is very clear, when he pens this scripture: "There is neither Jew nor Gentile, neither slave nor free, nor is there male and female, for you are all one in Christ Jesus (Galatians 3:28) NIV. However, this is why racism has been perpetuated because of so- called white Christians in power that think like the religious minded elderly female at Panera Bread. These type of individuals have the audacity to insist that a black and white person shouldn't be in a relationship; yet there isn't any scriptural support for their beliefs.

Moreover, I believe the aggression and callous acts against so many black males hinges on them having access to wealth and white women. This is why Hip-hop music and artists are hated amongst so many extremists. When it comes to criminality and social-ills, some like to disingenuously point the finger at the Hip-hop culture.

They always blame it on Hip Hop:

There's one particular Hip Hop artist by the name of Wyclef Jean, who wrote a hit song called, "The Industry." I must say that it's a profound song indeed. The Haitian- born artist sheds light on a bigger reality and reminds us that we can't blame everything that happens in urban or suburban settings on Hip-hop as so many try to do. Here are some words from the song:

> Shots go off, mother's cry
> Death since rise, homicide
> Black on black crime needs to stop
> Y'all can't blame it on hip hop

Cause what we say is what we see
What we see is reality
The ghetto's the ghetto you got them livin' in sorrow
Soon they won't live to see tomorrow!

The words go directly to the heart of socioeconomical issues and criminality in the black community. If I had to compare Hip-hip to an actual person, I would compare it to an unarmed urban-kid called Hip-hop wearing a Hoodie and walking down the street with a backpack from school. There are several examples of how this scenario plays out in America. It usually starts off with a neighborhood watch person or a regular civilian who has a suspicion about why the person is in their neighborhood. Then, the police get a call about a robbery and the urban-kid called Hip-hop is most likely mistaken for being the perpetrator, with no questions asked; the kid gets shot and killed. This is an example, of what the kid Hip-hop has to face just because of the minority component. Whereas, a suburban- white kid called (rock n roll or pop) can wear a Hoodie, enjoy his ice tea and skittles and never have to worry about racial profiling, stop and frisk, or unjustifiable un-armed shootings. Yes, black males get a 'bum'rap, blamed for the social- ills because of Hip hop music that expresses the reality of what they're exposed to everyday. This type of profiling must stop if we ever plan to move forward with true equality and solidarity in America.

Nonetheless, the industry is made of aristocratic, rich, white male CEOs, benefiting, distributing, and promoting commercial-ized Hip-hop. White CEOs benefit through record and CD sales, but we don't blame them or hold the distributors accountable for spreading seeds of violence though air and digital waves. Black males don't control the FCC and distribution, but they get blamed for their lyrical content, dialoging about "what they see as reality" while white producers and CEO's benefit from the CD sales as well.

The fact is, Hip-hop was underestimated and miscalculated by white America. The music has gone from a genre to a culture that is impacting white kids as well. I believe this is why black males artist are hated because of the influence of Hip-hop on suburban white kids as well. The conservatives and racists love to redirect everyone's attention to what they call "hazardous hip hop" when "shots go off!" However, America established its prosperity, control, slavery and colonialism through violence. For instance, growing up I watched white men in big hats, kill indigenous Indians. I thought it was just raw entertainment and I didn't know it was a part of America's history of colonization and enslavement. I believe, it is hypocritical to blame Hip-hop artists in regards to violence, when in fact, this nation was established through violent control. For example, if an insolent, alcoholic, dad beats his wife in front of his kids, one day, his kid will grow up and mimic such behavior. Well, this is the case of America and its so- called illegitimate urban-kid called (Hip hop). It has mimicked the behavior of his illegal guardian (America). This country has displayed domestic and foreign violence through law enforcement and war mistreating minorities in particular.

Moreover, conservatives and racists need to just stop being disingenuous and blaming many 'inner city blues and social- ills on Hip hop as well as stop using euphemisms like (thugs and gangsters). These are all terms and replacement language that hide a much bigger problem. There is disdain for black males; and every now and then, true feelings manifest about black males through racist rhetoric or unarmed shootings. Michael Ralph states: "There was the persecution rap music faced during the 1990s, when the U.S. Congress debated its detrimental effects amid a moral panic that viewed inner-city gangbangers and drug dealers as obstacles to American democracy and decency" (Ralph, 2009). There goes that J. Edgar Hoover assessment of black males again. The terminology that congress uses about "inner city gangbangers" and "drug dealers" being obstacles to American democracy, stems from historical hatred. Instead of using direct language of racism, white males in high places like congress, use euphemisms to hide what they really think. The fact is, people like those in congress are threatened by black males having too much power through art forms of expression like Hip-hop. I believe It all comes down to "power" and "control" and Hip-hop gives black males that, but racist individuals become intimidated and start implementing task forces connecting black males to criminality. After all, to see a Hip hop artist in a hundred thousand dollar vehicle while you drive something economical is disheartening for some or to have a black male living in your aristocratic community would make anti- Hip hop pundits upset and fearful. This is what I derive from the congressman's statement in the article. He and others fear black males having access to wealth, white women, and the minds of their white kids. Well,... I just have four words for Americas' phobia... "You are too damn late!"

The fear of real black power:

I believe wealth and influence is wonderful for so many of our successful black men and women. However, there's something that young black males should consider while enjoying a slice of the American pie, and that something is what Dr. Claud Anderson (1994) mentions in his book: Black Labor, White Wealth, called: "Vertical integration" (p. 208). In the concept of "vertical integration", a single entity or group controls all aspects of creation and sale of a service or product. Historically, whites have manipulated blacks physical gifting through slave breeding. Though blacks have been become successful artists, they have failed to access or control the money generated by the music industry (Anderson, 1994).

This is an awesome assessment and I agree with Mr. Anderson. I believe that the prosperity and popularity are legitimate achievements for so many young black males. However, today Blacks need to be aware of supervised power and white notoriety because it is no different than historical servility, especially when there are contemporary slave master's lording over black progress and prosperity. The pimp and prostitute scenario still plays out in the long-run because America is industrially pimping, at the expense of so many minorities, through industries such as sports, entertainment, music, and even mass incarceration. The Hip-hop movement is wonderful and has made more strides to reaching generations than any historical movement. Yet, black leadership has failed to articulate and educate young black males, love them, and educate them on the importance of "vertical integration (Anderson, 1994).

Most of all, many in black leadership have failed to exhort our young success stories to think and to do business like Oprah Winfrey and Tyler Perry. Yes, when transacting in the market places of America, black men and women should hold America accountable concerning their place value; they should challenge America's threat- list and demand equality and quality. If systematic America desires black talent, but refuse to treat us as equals; I believe threatening to build and buy from black owned businesses is necessary.

Action steps:

1. More black leaders need to articulate "vertical integration" by (Dr. Claud Anderson) and stress the importance of donating to HBCU's.
2. Supporting the "Black farm struggle" is key as well.
3. Knowing our Civil ordinances and Constitutional rights will create a social buffer from unlawful searches and unreasonable force.

Yes, as black males reach a certain pinnacle of success in the American empire, we should be cognizant of the *Caste* systems that Michelle Alexander talks about in her book, *The New Jim*

Crow, (2010-12). We should be aware about the 'violation of ordinances in America because when you violate laws, and one day, you may, you will be quickly reminded of your place value through stop and frisk, unjustifiable shootings, and modern day prosecutorial lynching. Yes, systematic America will give you a fresh dose of *Mass incarceration in the age of color blindness (*Alexander, 2010-2012*)*. Remember, when you violate ordinances, your pistols, prosperity, and popularity won't matter because systematic America will strip you of yourself, wealth and... that damn Hoodie!

CHAPTER THREE

THAT DAMN HOODIE!

"The reason Trayvon Martin died is because he looked a certain way, and it wasn't based on skin color, but he was wearing a Hoodie, and he looked a certain way, and that way is how gangstas look. And therefore he got attention!"

-Bill O'Reilly-

The above-mentioned disingenuous assessment made by Mr. O'Reilly in regards to the slain teenager, Trayvon Benjamin Martin, was from an interview conducted with an African American conservative, Allen West. The 2012' killing of 'Trayvon Martin has gained national attention and divided the nation, especially, when it comes to racial profiling and unarmed shootings of black males. I am appalled at Mr. O'Reilly's disingenuous statement that the reason Trayvon Martin died was because he looked a certain way", and that it wasn't based on skin color" (Huff Post, 2013). I like to consider Mr. O'Reilly a Pinhead; this is something he often uses during his weekly broadcast when he doesn't agree with certain pundits. I do vehemently agree with certain aspects of his assessment, but disagree with the majority of his critique.

I agree that the reason Trayvon Martin died is because he looked a certain way, "a black male". During the interview with Mr. West, Mr. O'Reilly goes on to suggest a more acceptable dress code, one that he believes will proof young black males from being racially profiled, stopped and frisked, or even unjustifiably shot. He says, "If Trayvon Martin had been wearing a jacket like you or a tie,...Mr. West, I don't think George Zimmerman would've had any problem with Mr. Martin". The problem with Mr. O'Reilly's anecdotal and post- assessment is that on the night of Mr. Martin's death, it was cold and sprinkling. Secondly, George Zimmerman didn't stress the attire of Trayvon Martin; he was concerned that previous burglaries had taken place and that the culprits where black males. This is a classic case of racial profiling that went terribly wrong. A young seventeen-year-olds life was taken for no reason at all, except that he was a Hoodie wearing black male that crossed paths with a man who was a liar and a loose cannon.

The fact is that black males are often criminalized for the way they look or what they wear regardless of who they really are on the inside. The statement by Mr. O'Reilly, and other conservative pundits are disingenuous at heart. Black men who have PHDs, own their own businesses, or drive nice cars have been racially profiled. For example, according to one particular article, "Colorism" is alive and well in America.

The article states:

> Sometimes a black man is racially profiled against because of the way he is dressed. An airport detention that led to the arrest of a person who fit the description of a money courier. They also stated that the person who was arrested in the investigation was a Black man. The black man was flamboyantly dressed and was wearing heavy gold jewelry. There was a white man, who was an attorney, who was dressed the same way as the black man, but wasn't arrested for loitering around in the airport for several hours. The defense argued that everything was equal, except race, and has proven that the white man was not questioned, and the black man was detained because of the color of his skin (Byers, 2013).

The article is clear that black males are profiled and their attire is just a technicality. Case in point, I remember doing some cabinetry and millworks for a customer in Fontana, California. I had a pretty nice 1997 black Ford-150 with my company logo posted on the side along with my contractor's license number. My registration, insurance, and vehicle were up to date. A white law enforcement officer pulled me over; he said that the reason why he pulled me over is because of the drug activity problem on that particular street. I didn't get mad at that possible fact, but then he made me get out of my truck, sit on the curb, and wait thirty minutes while he ran my information. This made me quite angry, but I kept my composure. My point is that racist cops do profiling based on skin color, not just clothing. Mr. O'Reilly is very assumptive and delusional to think that George Zimmerman wouldn't have had a problem with Mr. Martin if Trayvon had on his Sunday best.

Moreover, the problem is our honor roll system in America along with the negative stigmas that are placed on black males. The truth is that America dishonors the black male, criminalizes, and associates him with every negative depiction which was initiated early in American history. For example, in the Jesse Washington's lynching of May of 1916, it was savages, gangster's, thugs, angry, and inferior white males whom acted out their abnormal aggression on black males in the worst of ways, including lynching's. It is very important for white males to study our history, noting the hypocrisy and perpetuations of racism against the black male. I believe this will allow them to see that thugism started with their predecessors, and countless cold case murders of black males which remain a mystery at the hands of white men wearing hoods across the South and beyond.

A little history of the Hoodie:

When it comes to head coverings there's significant history, but criminalization was never directed towards Anglican individuals or groups for their choice of attire. However, in ancient cultures head coverings, the Hoodie was part of rituals and worn causally.

For instance, the Semitic culture of Hebrews and Jews wore head coverings. During the time of Jesus, Jewish teachers always had their heads covered in public as a sign of righteous reverence. They apparently wore the "sudarium," a white linen cloth, wound round the head as a turban with the ends of it falling down over the neck. Common people sometimes wore a cloth with a band or just a band in warm months. The term cloak is a term used as well to describe head coverings. According to Gower (2005), he states, "A cloak or mantle was worn on top of the tunic, when cold weather made it necessity a cloak or mantle was worn (Gower, 2005).

In addition, there were several cultic groups like Monastic's, Templar's, and Crusaders. Let's not forget, the modern group, "Ku Klux Klan", wore hoods during "knight rides" and lynching's of countless black males and females. All of a sudden, on a drizzling night, an African American male by the name of Trayvon Benjamin Martin wore a Hoodie and it became a symbol of criminalization. This is so hypocritical of some people in America to suggest that black males wearing a Hoodie are engaging in some criminal act. This is what Mr. O'Reilly and his conservative pundits purposed about Trayvon Benjamin Martin. Michelle Alexander makes an excellent point juxtaposing differences in how we perceive an urban kid versus his white counterparts in regards to criminality.

Alexander states:

> "Who should we fear? The kid in the hood who joined a gang and now carries a gun for security because his neighborhood is frightening and unsafe? Or the suburban high school student who has a drinking problem, but keeps getting behind the wheel (Alexander, 2012-2102)?

Stereotypes influence the opinions of people which cause them to look at people a certain way. I believe the media depicts negative stereotypes of black males wearing certain attire in a criminal context which causes us to automatically fear and assume that the black male is more likely to commit a crime. Mr. O'Reilly's assessment of what is appropriate dress code for black males is whimsical, but disingenuous. It doesn't matter what a black male wears; he'd still likely be racially profiled in color-coded America.

For example, the NFL has some staggering statistics on black football players being racially profiled; one particular case has drawn quite a bit of attention:

The report recounts the case of Matthias Askew who, after being spotted by Cincinnati police, was singled out, harassed, and arrested after a minor parking violation, even though he hadn't committed a crime. "They tased him simply because he was a big black man, not because he did anything to make them fear for their safety" (Racial Profiling: NFL Players, 2013). This case shows how out of control white law enforcement agents are when it comes to the criminality and brutality of even successful black males. If you're still not convinced about this prevailing issue here are some statistics.

> In a league in which 66% of the players are black and 31% are white, black players were arrested nearly 10 times as often as white players," of the 687 total player arrests, 607 involved black players. That's a whopping 88 percent (Racial Profiling: Black NFL Players Get Arrested 10 Times as Often as Whites, 2013).

Wow, a whopping 88% is unacceptable. While Mr. O'Reilly believes a suit and tie are the anecdote to end or suppress racial profiling of so many black males; the problem is not just clothing, but colorism. I believe the changing of one's attire to suit the acceptability of white America still wouldn't be enough conformity. The fact is that black males are not valued, regardless of their clothing. It's amazing, how some white theorists and psychologists come up with all kinds of empathic excuses for white males that misbehave. There's so much sympathy for the sons of America, white males; yet black males are labeled and criminalized for any misbehavior and hauled off to a state or federal facility.

Furthermore, black males are criminalized for wearing certain clothing (Hoodie); while their white counterparts are glorified; especially for portraying a thug or a gangster in movies. For instance, Hollywood will cast a white male in a dark and sinister role(s), but the scene will be created in such a way that the audience will get emotional, but not angry with the white villain. I saw this in the movie, Training Day, starring Denzel Washington, and Ethan Hawk. Denzel was a dirty cop, but Ethan Hawk was a new recruit, whose role was very likeable. In Brooklyn's Finest, Ethan Hawk played a struggling cop that compromised some ethic guidelines. He lived in an asbestos prone apartment, which made his wife sick. He wanted a better life for his wife and kids, so he put on a Hoodie, and decided to steal drug money from dealers to help move his wife and kids to a better place. My point is, when Mr. Hawk's character was killed off, Hollywood made the audience feel empathy for the white male playing a compromised cop during the white actor's fate.

America has a fascination with blaxploitation, but when it comes to "Save the World or empathy films," why is there always a white male as the likely figure to Don such roles? Ironically, America's history tells a different story because without black males and females slaving in cotton and tobacco fields, and fighting in wars, the currency and conquest in this country would've been unobtainable and unconquerable. This is why films like The Tuskegee Airmen, Glory, and Red Tails rose to the surface. Thankfully, a handful of black filmmakers researched and demanded that the truth be told about the sacrifices and contributions of black men and women in this country.

Growing up, I remember watching a white Italian gangster by the name of Al Capone. He dressed in nice suits and drove a clean classic car, but he sold bootlegged liquor, spearheaded drive-by shootings, and killed rival mobsters. America glorified and romanticized white thugism, and the following article addresses America's passivity toward this type of white male thugism.

The article states:

> He was America's first celebrity criminal (Al Capone), all this was clear to much of the nation, not just to Chicagoans. Federal prosecutors charged Capone not with running illegal breweries or selling whiskey or even slaughtering rival mobsters, but with failure to pay his income taxes (Richman, 2005).

This is shocking how Federal prosecutors didn't charge him with illegal breweries or murdering rivals, but with tax invasion. The fact that a suit wearing...white gangster is romanticized by Americans; can set up a criminal enterprise and commit domestic terrorism, but only get charged with "tax invasion" is astounding. Whereas, a Hoodie wearing, black male gets criminalized for his clothing and color; racially profiled, stopped and frisked, and even killed for simply being black in America; this is unacceptable. The unfair assessment of Mr. O'Reilly and many other conservative pundits on the Hoodie issue is downright dangerous and contributes to more dehumanization of black males. Too much of the attention was taken off of a slain teenager (Trayvon B. Martin) and placed on an inanimate object, a twenty to thirty dollar Hoodie.

That Hoodie stole the show:

I must say that it was a shame how the Hoodie on display during the Trayvon Martin trial was given more attention than justice for the slain teen. A Hoodie with a blood stain and a single gunshot hole was placed into evidence and displayed in court for the public to see. The Hoodie was so much of the center of attention that we've forgotten that an innocent black male was executed. The system allowed a murderer to go free because the life of a black male was not valued when a Hispanic white man said that he feared for his life. Mr. Martin's character was put on trial and associated with a thirty-dollar Hoodie using an all white jury. One of the jurors, the foreman, said something that was questionable. Though, she was forward and frank during her CNN interview, she was highly criticized by many.

According to Juror B-37:

> "It was Zimmerman's voice on the recording. "All but probably one" of the jurors believed the screams were Zimmerman, according to the juror, "because of the evidence that he was the one that had gotten beaten." "He's learned a good lesson," she "would feel comfortable having George" on her neighborhood watch (Huff Post Black-Voice, 2013)

I've watched the entire interview on CNN and must say that my mouth hit the floor while this small town, White woman legalistically robbed the Martin's family of justice . She had so much empathy for George Zimmerman, one would have thought she was Zimmerman's birth mom. My point is that this particular jury was so adamant about George Zimmerman being the victim in this case, and not the culprit that they set him free. She believed, "He learned a good lesson." Her language and demeanor was extremely emphatic towards Mr. Zimmerman. I've learned about Interpersonal communication, that an individual can reveal a lot about themselves through body language, his or her demeanor or euphemisms. Juror B-37 had a sour spirit about her that gave me concern. I believe she was a subliminal racist and that she used the system to practice her personal biases at the expense of a murdered black teen. The bottom line is that jury selection in this country hasn't change a bit. The jury box is never balanced, especially for blacks on trial. The day of the verdict, America watched a murderer go free.

In addition, I believe Juror B-37 came into this case with a presupposition about young black males. Based on her emotionality towards Zimmerman, she never considered Trayvon Benjamin Martin as the victim. She didn't consider the power of a gun, in the hands of a grown man, shooting an unarmed seventeen-year-old as something criminal. She didn't believe that a Hoodie wearing teenager feared for his life and was only responding in a manner that Sigmund Freud considers a "fight or flight" response. Trayvon Martin tried to get away from the stranger, George Zimmerman, or in Rachel Jentel's words, "A creepy ass cracker."

It is clear to many that Mr. Zimmerman predatorily pursued Trayvon Martin and killed him like he was a deer in the wild. Jury B-37 didn't consider this a possibility or probability; she was determined to get George Zimmerman off for murder, and he did get off. I don't respect her as a juror, but at least she gave us a glimpse of what America thinks about black males. People like Juror B-37 and America doesn't consider humanistic qualities when looking upon black males. In their minds, the black male is just a Hoodie wearing, Hip-hop head, thug, and weed smoking liability. For instance, some racist will give bias assessments like Heather Mac Donald; National Review writer, she believes: "Black males lack "impulse control" in which leads to such high crime rates among young Black males inevitably means more disruptive behavior in school" (Gaynor, 2014). This type of assessment and language is counterproductive and create more disdain that already exist for black males. These are euphemisms used by people like Bill O'Reilly, conservative pundit, and white racist Americans. I believe this was the mindset of Juror B-37. She didn't show concern or place value for Trayvon Martin's life or his death. The critics will ask, "How could you tell what her mindset was?" A racist doesn't have to call a minority a derogatory term, but he or she can treat, cheat, and withhold resources, opportunities, justice or freedom. That can be just as sinister as criminalizing or calling someone a derogatory term.

Action steps:

1. Young black males should consider pulling up their pants to avoid criminalization, racial profiling and other grim outcomes.

2. Clothing can be worn in a cordial manner because there are too many young men with their pants hanging off their behinds, drawing unnecessary attention from racist cops that doesn't value black males.

2. I believe pervasive protest should be non- negotiable during injustices. It seems that the current injustices disproportionality warrants a call to action through peaceful demonstrations.

Sadly, justice didn't flow down like a mighty stream for Trayvon Benjamin Martin. The verdict is indicative of America's perception of the black male; the verdict suggests that black males are a disgrace and deserving of injustice as well as displacement by any means necessary.

CHAPTER FOUR

The Happening of Black America

"Cruel and abusive whites created sports that used blacks like footballs or ducks, to entertain themselves and make money, whites developed a games called 'coon hunting'"

-Dr. Claud Anderson-

Disgracing a whole culture:

The behavior of white slave masters in the South was most appalling, and so many young black males need to understand the horrendous acts against our predecessors. The disgracing of black males through "Coon hunting" was a sick game indeed, but it shows that white slave masters were not only cruel, but obviously had too much time on their hands. There is nothing entertaining about killing another human being, but hunting down and killing black males was definitely a sport in the antebellum South.

According to Dr. Anderson (1994):

> A slave with whom a white owner was dissatisfied was covered with a scent and set free to run in the woods at night. The slave holders released their hound dogs to track and tree the slave. Bets would be placed as to whose dogs would catch the slave first. Once caught, the slave was usually shot from the tree like a raccoon (p.216).

It seems that the hunting and killing of black males was a

sport, and this ugly piece of history is significant for us in the twenty first century as well. It's important because during the Riot in the 1960s, white law enforcement agents used high pressure water hoses and hounds on black citizens that were dissatisfied with racism and police brutality. I believe "Coon hunting" is still practiced through law enforcement tactics and the hounds (K-9's) are choice methods to hunt and sniff out urban criminals, far too often minorities. However, for African Americans that migrated from the South and presided in Los Angeles, the 1960's was a reminder of the old "Jim Crow" agenda that impacted African Americans. The LAPD played a major role in disgracing of black and brown citizens. I believe so many young black males gang members, (Crips and Bloods,) are not aware of the racism that existed in Los Angeles, CA during the fifties and sixties. It wasn't just in the South that Jim Crowism had taken place, but Southern racists migrated as well; instituting tactical and radical enforcement against minorities. The military- like force brought William Parker's LAPD heavy criticism from the city's Latino and black residents for brutality. Police had a habit of beating minorities, and intimidating them in a similar manner as the Klan in the South. Chief Parker was known for the term Thin Blue line. His philosophy was to establish a presence in urban areas and dominance while they were still young and show them who was boss. This racist behavior of the Chief and many officers instigated injustices and resulted in the Watts riot on August 11, 1965 (Wikipedia, 2013).

The "Watts riot" was an outcry against police brutality and socioeconomical disparity. Some critics have the nerve to say, "Those blacks involved in the riot were acting uncivilized and tearing up their own neighborhood". The Los Angeles police Chief, Parker, publicly described the people he saw involved in the riots as acting like "monkeys in the zoo".

This is an example of another white male in systematic America, using a euphemism and code language for hidden racist dogma. The epithet "Monkeys in a zoo" is another way of expression the "N" word amongst other racist garbage directed towards blacks. I believe when a racist, anti-black figure, is in such a position as Chief of police, there 's going to be social upheaval, inequality and injustice. Chief Parker made sure he disgraced as many young blacks as possible based *on* his philosophy to intimidate young black males by letting them know who's the boss. The behavior of Mr. Parker is still displayed by many white law enforcement agents across America. I believe this is why there's been so many cases of racial profiling, stop and frisk, and unarmed shootings of black males. As a nation, we have adopted and implemented Chief Parker's ideology of 'showing the black male who is boss' by allowing the practice of pervasive racism; the Chief and his kind has managed to bring over from the old, dirty, South. Chief Parker, J. Edgar Hoover, and several others are responsible for the disgracing of so many of black males. The pervasive tactics of such individuals and institutions has been the culprit for the destruction and displacement of a generation of men through unarmed shootings and mass incarceration. This maladaptive behavior has also been a contributing factor of the displacement of many black men and culprit for the single- parent problem in the black community.

The Black men-(MIA) Myth:

Some have suggested that black men are lazy, heartless or simply "Missing In Action" (MIA), especially, when it comes to family and socioeconomical rank. One particular finding hampers previous notions about black males as not involved in their families and communities. Based on new data, by The Centers for Disease Control and Prevention (CDC), the black family is much more complete than is widely perceived. Being a father myself, the recent results are refreshing, especially in the case of Black fathers who have been written off as absent or simply just sperm donors.

Here's snapshots from the study:

Among children under the age of five, Black men not in the house-hold are more likely than other fathers who live with their kids to eat with their children every day.

For parents of children under the age of five, Black men were more likely than white and Hispanic fathers who DO NOT live with their kids to eat with them every day.

Among fathers unable to live with their children in the household with kids under the age of five, black men were more likely than dads from other ethnic groups to bathe their kids daily.

Among parents with kids under the age of five, black men were more likely to read to their children daily.

Among children above the age of five, black men were more likely to make sure their kids did their homework. This is true whether or not they lived with the child.

Among parents of children above the age of five, black men were more likely to talk to their child about their day.

(Kulture Kritic, 2014).

Based on the study, there are black men doing the best they can with what they have to work with. I'm a traditional family kind of guy who idealistically believes in two-parent homes; we do need more complete families and not incomplete households in the African America community as well . The study suggests that black men are involved and active in the lives of their children. This is why a keen understanding is necessary for young black males to-day, in regard to previous groups of black men like the Black Panther's party whom were instrumental in the establishing of the black community in the sixties. The BPP and other African American groups were ostracized and demonized by white power structures and disassembled through deadly force, causing disruption in the balk family, community, and socioeconomical opportunities. For example, one particular article addressed the position of the Black Panther party's member, Huey Newton.

Tyner, (2006):

In 1969, for example, he explained that

> Because African Americans lack political power, Black people are not free" formation of the Black Panther Party occurred, therefore, because "We began. . . by checking around with the street brothers. We asked them if they would be interested in forming the Black Panther Party for Self-Defense, which would be based upon defending the community against the aggression of the power structure, including the military and the armed might of the police" (Tyner, 2006).

Black men like Mr. Newton and others were fed up with police brutality, powerlessness and decided to stir every black male in their communities in an effort to defend their communities against racism. I see no problem in self-defense or organizing a group to fortify and edify one's community. Mr. Newton and other black men were not terrorists, but J. Edgar Hoover, ex- head of the FBI, set up a special taskforce, COINTELPRO, to disgrace a group of strong, educated black men. Mr. Hoover considered such groups and individuals as "The greatest threat to the internal security of the country" (Wikipedia, 2013). The hate for this group of black men was baseless and senseless. The real threat to America was and is racism. The BPP was a group of black males that were just trying to value their community through worthy causes and programs. For instance, The BPP did some positive things in the community including the following: the Survivor Programs, Free Breakfast for Children Program, free services such as clothing distribution, classes on politics and economics, free medical clinics, lessons on self-defense and first aid, transportation to upstate prisons for family members of inmates, an emergency response ambulance program, drug and alcohol rehabilitation, and testing for sickle-cell disease. The BPP also founded the "Intercommunal Youth Institute" in January 1971, with the intent of demonstrating how black youth ought to be educated. This BPP were an active group of men in their communities. Based on their agenda, I don't believe the BPP displayed an ounce of a 'National threat. Those black men were concerned about progress in their own community and just trying to survive. White power structures in America made sure groups like the BPP didn't flourish during the sixties.

Moreover, one particular day I had an exchange with one of my white professors during my graduate program. The professor made a suspicious statement during a diversity topic, he said: "I just don't see any African American male mentors out there." He didn't give any specifics, he simply stated his opinion. One other gentleman and myself were the only African American males in the class of predominantly white and a few Asian students. The classroom was silent for a few seconds, but I felt I had an obligation to respond. I began to share the pivotal time and movement of the Black Panther Party (BPP). My response to him was: "Well, historically, there have been organizations like the BPP that consisted of strong and educated black males whom implemented programs (Survivors Program). However, white males in power like J. Edgar Hoover criminalized and exterminated them. "With all respect sir, the sixties was a pivotal era for black males because the group and movement would've leveled the playing field- educationally, and socio economically for us; however, white racist males in power made sure that those black males didn't prosper in the sixties and beyond." The classroom went silent again, but of course, the professor went into defense mode; however, you can't refute historical truth.

Moreover, there are disingenuous individuals and groups in America that espouse the notion that 'there are no black male mentors. However, when it comes to 'the ugly side of America (racism and the devaluing of black males), these individuals get amnesia or suffer from a disorder that I call (white- denial). They deny that 'race still has a place in America. They disgrace the black race with criminalized assessments, and fail to acknowledge the accomplishments and contributions of so many black males like: Earvin Magic Johnson (athlete and entrepreneur), Nation Of Islam (reached and rehabilitated many black males), Bill Cosby (awesome financial contributions to HBCU's), Steve Harvey (has an at risk boys mentoring program), and Russell Simmons (Hip hop mogul and entrepreneur), Dr. Steve Perry (the principal of Capital Preparatory Magnet School) etc. These are just a few but there are a host of others mentoring and supporting their communities . Personally, I believe the intent of my professor and his assessment didn't come from a place of endearment. The fact is that he and other white males in positions of power don't want to see black male mentors economically or educationally proficient because that will produce jobs and a shift in power for black males when white males have been dominant in this country. I doubt very seriously that he and his colleagues would make room for, protest or rally to hire black males where he works or elsewhere. However, individuals like him are so adamantly vocal about the plight of the black male, without ever presenting any authentic solutions or admitting America's role in the systematic disassembling , devaluing, and demonizing of black males.

In addition, there are untold or overlooked truths like the Wilmington on Fire incident in 1898. The documentary by Chris Everett, is significant because it parrots the 1960's BPP movement. The story is one that fell through the cracks and isn't often mentioned when speaking about historic events, in regards to black progress and success. The event that took place was so impactful that even today blacks are still feeling the repercussions of that brutal attack.

Greg. B, (2013) States:

> The story of the Wilmington massacre of 1898 goes as such; prior to the civil war, Wilmington had 10,000 blacks and was a thriving community. The port in Wilmington served as a means for employment, and trade (The Bloody Massacre of Blacks in Wilmington).

The fact is Blacks became prominent in Wilmington and with this came an election where a white mayor and a bi-racial city council was elected. The sad reality is two days later, a Democratic party of white supremacists 1500 strong and full of white men, ran community leaders out of the city and burned black businesses.

This is what my professor and many others don't seem to take into consideration when assessing the black male. In this Wilmington town, black males were in the forefront of economical success, but what happened? Racism happened. A bunch of white males "1500 strong" were inferior and full of rage, attacked the town and annihilated that black community, in Wilmington, NC (1898). The fact is that any time black males were in their 'rightful place, there were angry white men obstructing black progress, and attacking black communities.

In addition, it would be counterintuitive on my part, if I didn't mention another era of black male leadership and progress being thwarted by white on, black crime. Black Wall Street was established by a Black man O.W. Gurley, a wealthy African American land-owner who hailed from Arkansas; in 1889 he purchased 40 acres of land in Tulsa, Oklahoma. Black Wall Street included successive businesses, churches, restaurants, grocery stores, two movie theaters, a hospital, bank, post office, libraries, schools, two airports, and a bus system (Spivey Y., 2013). This was a self contained empire that had been established by blacks. However, on June 01, 1921, a race riot prevailed by the KKK and black progress was annihilated.

This is a low down-dirty shame, on racist America's part that the success and legacy of Mr. Gurley was interrupted by racism. The black community seems to be always under siege or surveillance by angry white males in power or seeking more control. Reflecting back to my white professor's assessment of "No black male role models" I believe there's a shortage because racism has claimed the lives and incarcerated a whole culture of men.' As a nation, we have the audacity to blame most of the social ills in the black community on absentee fathers. Yes, having a father in the home is important because kids are more likely to do better in school and society, and less likely to engage in social anarchy. There is a pandemic in regards to 'sex, drugs, and rock' n roll in the African American community as well. If there were more African American fathers in the home, a lot of children would overcome identity, belonging and self esteem issues. The fact is children from fatherless homes are more likely to suffer from psychological, emotional and social issues, drop out of school and face incarceration according to a University of Michigan study(Krout, 2013).

I included the probability because I wanted systematic America to realize her role in these odds for black children. When historical cases like the Wilmington Fire, Black Wall Street, and the Black Panther Party (BPP) had black people terrorized and annihilated, the black community suffered most in 'the fatherhood department. The BPP was initially a group of black males (fathers, husbands, and dads), and by annihilating them, systematic America attacked the role of the black male in the home and community. This set the African American community back for years. The historical attacks on the black male and his family created the very outcomes and social ills espoused in the statistics mentioned. However, this wasn't enough because a new attack on black males was forged, one that was more industrial, which displaced a whole culture of men. The prison industrial complex has served as a post-modern form of slavery and has housed more black men and women than any other ethnic group.

Displacing of black males:

The courtrooms across America play a major role in the displacing of black males through over prosecutorial practices and mass incarceration. I was watching CNN when defense attorney, Mark Geragos said something profound. He said, 'race plays a part in courtrooms and black males are automatically presumed guilty when they enter a courtroom *(Geragos, 2013)*. I agree. And in supporting Mr. Geragos statement: I hired an attorney for my youngest son's case, an incident that got 'blown out of proportion at his high school. The school's vice Principal (white male) didn't do a proper investigation of the allegations made against my fifteen- year- old son. Instead, the vice Principal called in a local law enforcement agent (white male), and my son found himself accused of a felony. The attorney I hired parroted Mr. Geragos statement, telling my son, "You're a black male and you're automatically presumed guilty when you walk inside that courtroom. So when the judge speaks to you, respond: "Yes or no, your honor." This is a white, Italian man admitting to what kind of odds black males face in systematic America, especially, in a court of Law; black males' freedom is often hijacked by over prosecutorial practices.

According to Michelle Alexander, (p. 219), she says:

> No longer needed to pick cotton in the fields or labor in factors, lower case black men were hauled off to prison in droves. They were vilified in the media and condemned for their condition. Decades later, curious onlookers in the grips of denial would wonder aloud, "Where have all the

black men gone? (Alexander, 2010-2012)

Mrs. Alexander proves my point, to my white professor earlier about the shortage of black male role models. "Where have all the black males gone?" is preciously the bewilderment of some that are dumfounded or downright disingenuous about the racist happening in Black America. According to *Color of Change*, It's reported that *The United States of America imprison more people than any other country in the world with Black men being affected the greatest* (Spivey B. Y., 2013).

I believe history and statistics are important because, they tell us something about the pattern and personality of a system's intent. Some may call this a conspiracy theory, but the disparities and fatalities don't suggest that I'm hallucinating. After all, look at what happened to the Black Panther Party (BPP) and other groups of black men who were fed up with inequality and injustice; destruction and mass incarceration were the end results. Far too often, black males are "vilified" when they decide to do for self, organize, and stand in their "rightful place". They're considered gangsters, thugs, and radicals when they congregate, whereas other cultures of men are considered hard working, valued, and even preferred over the black male. The sheer hatred for black males has permeated the cognition of so many white males in power. One particular white male, a senator tweeted something very controversial but subliminally racist at heart. Rep. Pat Garofalo, R-Farmington, tweeted. "Let's be honest, 70% of teams in NBA could fold tomorrow nobody would notice a difference w/ possible exception of increase in street crime" (Breaking Brown, 2014). This is a law maker making such bias assessments, and this is a good example of how most white males in power positions feel about black males in sports and entertainment. He is talking about street crime, but doesn't mention "racially motivated" incidents of police brutality that take place on a daily basis against black men across the nation.

In all fairness, there is enough 'blame to go around for the devaluing that takes place; and we've brought some of this treatment on ourselves. This brings me to another point about self-hatred; the "plantation personality" or what is suggested to be the "House versus field negro" mentality amongst so many black males. The divisive behavior amongst some blacks has found its way into political America and it has definitely not contributed to the progress or unification of black folks.

Discoloration: predicable vs. unpredictable Negros

In all honesty, when it comes to likeability or un-likeability in America, there have been labels and stigmatization in the black community that are not befitting. The labels have not come from racist whites only, but self-hated has allowed terms like "House Nigger and uncle Tom" to devalue the black community as well. Now this type of labeling is understandable because some have behaved like Steven in the movie *Django,* parachuting their way into white notoriety. Historically, racist America has had certain preferences for the type of Negro she is willing to notarize such as The predictable Negro (Butler), while criminalizing and imprisoning others that don't comply or retrofit their way into servile roles in society.

America's most effective method for ensuring enmity between black males is through the old "plantation personality." The predictable Negro, is considered to be the (Butler) type. He or she is a more accepted individual because they seem to be non- threatening or non-radical, and easy to indenture into servile roles in America. Some may consider this type of Negro: conservative, patriotic, or tea party affiliated. He or she is most likely to be highly proficient in conservative politics, adamant about the U.S. Constitution, dismissive of his or her own Afro centricity/culture; and often found devaluing black males such as (hip hop artist, liberals and many other citizens in urban domains). Unfortunately, this type of individual(s) avoid racist America's role, function, and dysfunction; especially, when it comes to criminality and colorism. For instance, the mother of murdered teen Trayvon Benjamin Martin, "Sabrina Fulton's powerful and emotional plea to the National Urban League was scrutinized by a conservative Black token du jour, Crystal Wright, who has coined the moniker. Mrs. Wright on Twitter and attacked Mrs. Fulton as being opportunistic and dishonest. Mrs. Wright cruelly accused Fulton of "manufacturing a race war" and suggests that she "move on" or "get on with writing her book" (Savali, 2013).

Wow, this conservative female "chick" predictable Negro (Butleress), had the audacity to tell a traumatized black mother that lost her son to a senseless murder to "Move on, get on with writing her book." That's like a therapist crossing ethical guidelines of telling a fresh rape victim to 'move on and write a book about their experience as a coping mechanism.'

First and foremost, Mrs. Wright, "You're wrong and haven't earned the right to give an assessment of this grieving black mother's pain. Mrs. Wright doesn't qualify as a therapist or a psychologist to suggest how Mrs. Fulton should deal with the trauma of losing a child. Secondly, if Mrs. Fulton decides to write a book(s) about her trauma and son's death, she's certainly entitled to do so. Mrs. Wright is not the only black conservative to think and speak this way. In addition, there are other predictable Negro's that spew rhetoric or resort to the "plantation personality" against their own ethnic group. An African American male conservative by the name of Michael Massie seems to think that Trayvon Martin is responsible for his own death and that George Zimmerman was justified because he was legally allowed to carry a firearm.

Mr. Massie's states:

George Zimmerman shot and killed Martin because Martin was attacking and beating him. The ugly truth is just that simple. To raise the specter of skin color and to clothe the event in vestiges of radicalization and a zeitgeist of rampant racism is nothing more than an attempt to obfuscate that single, salient truth *(Massie, 2013)*.

Let me just point out that Mr. Massie wasn't there the night of the murder, but he sure sounds like a forensic expert on what happened the night Mr. Martin was murdered by Mr. Zimmerman. In his pro gun, anti- liberal mind, he seemed to have a revelation about the mind of Zimmerman. He believed that "Zimmerman did not kill Martin because of the color of his skin." Mr. Massie overlooked the fact that George Zimmerman's choice to follow and shoot Mr. Martin could have had a dichotomist component. Mr. Zimmerman could have killed Mr. Martin because he was losing the fight he started, and figured, a young black male was whooping his behind, so a bullet to the chest would make him the hero. There are no heroes when it comes to racism and violence. Mr. Massie is so 'conservative minded that he's no earthly good.' The fact is in Mr. Massie's words, "the single and salient truth" about what really happened that night is not obtainable; especially, when the only witness to the crime is a dead teenager Trayvon Benjamin Martin.

Furthermore, there is a disdain by some for this next type of individual called: The unpredictable Negro (Butcher). He or she is opposite of the predictable Negro (Butler). He or she is more liberal, threatening, radical and has fortitude: political, social, and religious. He or she undergirds the often ostracized and dehumanized (Hip hop culture and socially disenfranchised). The unpredictable Negro is not afraid to transition his voice into a social (Morris Berge), put it to the throat of racist America and demand equality and justice for all. For example Jeremiah Wright, President Barack Hussein Obama's ex- pastor, said something that made the earth stand still. He preached on America's hypocrisy and how America likes to petition heaven asking, God to bless America! The actual words brought him criticism, but were irrefutable, especially, when it comes to race in America.

Jeremiah Wright:

> The government gives them the drugs, builds bigger prisons, passes a three-strike law, and then wants us to sing "God Bless America." No, no, no. Not "God Bless America"; God Damn America! That's in the Bible, for killing innocent people! *(Weiss, 2008)*.

When this 'sound bite was played many patriotic whites and black conservatives and tea baggers were flabbergasted. Despite this sound bite being played 'over and over again by conservative pundits to derail Barack Obama's campaign for the presidency, the first- biracial president, in American history was still elected (twice). However, this political divisiveness seem to be a tactic that caused enmity between liberal and conservative blacks as well. The fact is white college kids turned out in record numbers and their vote is what helped placed President Barack Obama in the white house as well. However, younger whites are not the issues until they are coached by their white racist peers. There is a younger generation of whites that are fed up, but still older Southern whites control the power structures. I believe voting a biracial president into office is wonderful, but it will take at least another 50 -100 years before we see 'racism officially exorcised out of the American empire, hopefully.

Nonetheless, far too often, the problem with the "predictable Negro" is the false euphoria about his or her place value in systematic America. So many black conservatives buy into the notion that they are accepted and revered for their patriotism and love for this country. However, when it comes to loyalty and Constitutional matters white America will protect their social arrangements and the Constitution at any cost; even if it came down to sending us all back to Africa. It doesn't matter how loyal you are to this country or how willing you are to undergo the discolouration process to obtain white notoriety, the white power structures will not unbiasly respect or revere any Negro. You can bleach your skin, reject your own culture and acculturate into this society; you'll still be treated as an inferior being because of the color of your skin.

The fact is that every black person needs to understand America's historical and existential perception about the black male. It doesn't matter, if you're a black liberal or conservative, America believes the black male is a liability instead of an asset. I used "the predictable vs. the unpredictable Negro language to soften the blows of Malcolm X's "House Negro versus Field Negro comparison. This historical and existential hatred between certain blacks... has gone on too far... and needs to cease before we fulfill the desires of color-coded America by killing one another over white notoriety. This is why there's been a discoloration process and so many blacks reject their image and culture in order to be accepted into white America.

I love to cook and use stainless steel pots, but one day, I noticed some discoloration on my favorite pot. I had a brief revelation about discoloration in the black community. The definition for discoloration means the process of changing to a different, less attractive color or changing color in a bad way. Another definition says it can mean, "To undergo a change, become different in essence, losing its original nature" (Vocabulary.com). My point is that so many black men and women have exchanged or forfeited their love for their own culture, and this has created enmity between lighter and darker skinned blacks, liberal and conservative, educated and uneducated. This is why there's been a re-creation of the "plantation personality" or 'the setting of one against the other' see (Willie Lynch letter). Interestingly, Tyner (2006), addresses a notion about Northern and urban Negros. Rural, southern African Americans were seen as emblematic of long-suffering struggles, whereas the urban-based African Americans were portrayed in the media, in academia as pathological. She contends, for example, that "the activism of welfare mothers disappears from view because they cannot hold [a] place of American hero and symbol of national progress" (Tyner, 2006, p.108). The author mentions "national progress" as some trophy that some blacks feel is a necessity. I believe if "national progress" is accompanied by loss of identity, heritage, and culture (discolouration) that individuals should retain his or her success- receipt and return that pseudo form of progress ASAP.

There have been far too much enmity of "setting one against the other" amongst black Americans. This is why self- hatred and black on- black crime must stop because displacement and re- placement of black males seems to be the end game of color- coded America. If we examine the social arrangements and disparities, we can conclude that Anglican, Asian, and alternately Hispanic males are preferred and tolerated; while the black male finds himself on America's threat list or dishonor roll.

Furthermore, we have to ponder the question and ask, "Who is the real threat to America? Well, black males are not a threat because they have no social, religious, or political power. Historically and existentially, Anglican males have controlled the power structures in this country and even today with a bi-racial president presiding in the White House. White males still espouse political, religious, and socioeconomical rule. As far as I'm concerned, the threat to America is not black males, We have never been and don't desire to be. All we ever wanted is R-E-S-P-E-C-T, freedom and justice for all. For instance, there's a particular scene in the movie: *Amistad*, when an African slave by the name of Cinque, played by Djimon Hounsou, stretched out his chained hands and with tears in his eyes pleaded with the European magistrates by repeatedly saying, "Give us free" . This has been the earnest desire of black males (true freedom); not just freedom from Southern plantations, but freedom from stop and frisk, racial profiling and unjustifiable shootings. America, we want you to "Give us respect." Yes, respect is earned, but after four hundred years of slavery and blaxploitation... in the words of Minster Louis Farrakhan: "You owe us the damn country."

Actions steps:

1. We must cease from competing for white notoriety and cutting each other down in the streets and media.
2. Father and son relationships must be mended in the African American community as well.
3. Anger mismanagement is problematic amongst so many of black males due to poor father and son relationships. I believe there is too much masculinity and profanity that goes on between father and son relationships, but not enough humility and love language. Family prayer is something I conducted once a week in my home, and this discipline has kept me and my wife together for 22 years as well as my three sons ages18, 20, and 22 grounded and safe.
4. National Misconduct is problematic in our society as well. Far too many law enforcement agents engage in misconduct and need more than just sensitivity training., They need cultural competency training and an hour every week of person therapy to help them express and alleviate some of the frustrations that come with such jobs as being policemen.

Nonetheless, it seems that black males will continue being disgraced and displaced through criminality, mass incarceration, and unjustifiable shootings because America's 'unregenerate state hinders her in honoring the black male. As a result, we're are left with social perils that contribute to pre-orchestrated probabilities and a series of violent, inexplicable deaths across the nation of so many black men. Nevertheless, without further due, I'll cover this topic in the next chapter, addressing the "Probability of a black male."

CHAPTER FIVE

Probability of a Black Male!

"If I allow the fact that I am a Negro to checkmate my will to do, now, I will inevitably form the habit of being defeated!"

-Paul Revere Williams-

In America, I believe the reality for so many black males can be understood by presenting a mathematical analogy of probability. Interestingly, when calculating probability there 's three types of outcomes: basic, multiple independent, and complimentary events. In this chapter, I'll focus on a basic understanding of probability in regards to "racially motivated" outcomes. Also, there is another important component in mathematical symbols called "Order and inequality", and with an understanding of the less than ($<$), greater than($>$) or equal to ($=$) symbols, one can conclude logically on the issues of "race and inequality." I believe this method and symbolic meanings are significant for understanding systematic America's intent, in regards to the black male's place value. Unfortunately, America does not consider the value of the black male to be equal compared to his white, Asian, and alternatively Hispanic male counterpart.

Furthermore, I believe for the black male, the total sum of his plight has always been summed up in criminality, inequality, and unfortunately, fatality. There are statistics that support my claim and I will include that information shortly, but let's look at a scenario and decide if the black male lives in a society that values him or not. By the way, this scenario is a reality for many black men.

Scenario:

Let's assume three white males age (17-19), three black males age (17-19), and three Asians age (17-19), and three Hispanics age (17-19) are driving or chilling/hanging out. I use the age bracket of (17-19) because these numbers are the mean (average) and mode(frequency) of black males that's more likely to be stopped and frisked, racially profiled or un justifiable murdered by a law enforcement agent or gun wheeling white racist resorting to the "Stand Your Ground " law- like we saw in the Jordan Davis and Trayvon Martin cases.

Back to the scenario:

Let's assume, three- white males are in a nice Range Rover enjoying Monster drinks and listening to country music; and three Asians are in an Acura legend, heading towards a Cyber joint or something; and three black males are in a Range Rover, listening to Hip hop and the driver has on a hoodie or throwback jersey and the registration is current. Lastly, let's assume three Hispanics are in a SUV- Chevy Tahoe, listening to Hip hop or Mariachi music. Based on this scenario, what is the likelihood of the three- white males being randomly profiled, pulled over and frisked, or unjusti-fiably murdered by a white law enforcement agent for mistaken identity? Well, I believe for the white- males there would be a (0/3) chance, the Asians (0/3) chance, but the black male faces a definite (3/3) chance, and the Hispanics, a (2/3) chance. How do I know this? Because the probability and statistics suggests that a black male's odds are greater than any other ethnic group in America. According to Welch, (2007) studies on race and sentencing have shown that young Black males are sentenced more severely than are members of other racial or ethnic groups. Black males have to worry about the likelihood of being incarcerated seven times more than their White counterpart. Sadly, The odds that a Black man will do time at some point in his life is 1 in 3, but a white male's likeli-hood is only 1 in 25.

Furthermore, 1 in 3, is not a prefabricated probability, but a reality. So many black males have to live with these odds everyday of their lives. I remember driving to Sierra Madre, CA for a thir-teen-week group counseling session. The sessions were a require-ment for my Marriage & Family Therapist program (MFT), which gives students a feel for counseling settings and deal with counter-transference and transference issues before we are released to work in the field. One particular session was hostile between me and one white female, and the white facilitator. I blurted out "This is why, I was cautious about coming here because I know that race still has a place in America. This is why, I wore a dress shirt and a tie, instead of a Hoodie or throwback jersey." The facilitator and the rest of the group chuckled. The facilitator responded, "Bryant, I admire your courage to come here and share. She said, "I didn't know that this issue of race and racial profiling is that serious. Thanks for sharing. Really, from the bottom of my heart, I didn't know that you have to worry about wearing certain clothing to avoid being mistreated by certain people in the world." Besides that session, the experience ended on a good note.

I shared this because most white people don't think about or care about the daily probabilities black people face, black males in particular. There is a problem with cultural criminality in regards to assessing black males and their attire. Far too often, one's skin can be his or her sin... especially, if they're at the 'wrong place at a "white time". Moreover, there are disturbing cases like the Sean Bell incident that prove 'black males don't make it home' as often as their white counterparts. For example, In the morning hours of Nov. 25, 2006, Sean Bell, a twenty-three year old African Ameri-can, who lived in New York, was due to be married, but his future was cut short by a couple of white law enforcement agents. Mr. Bell left out of a Queens, NY strip, got into a Gray Nissan Altima with two male friends after celebrating for his bachelor's party.

Unfortunately, when the smoke settled Mr. Bell's sustained fifty bullets to his body at the hands of three law enforcement agents. Killing Mr. Bell wasn't enough. Judge Arthur J. Cooperman acquitted the police officers involved of all charges (Sean Bell, 2011). This is what most black males have to worry about across America. I'm a Los Angeles native and can share about the police brutality of most law enforcement agents towards black males, but I've heard cops in cities like New York are sinister also, especially, when it comes to racial profiling and police brutality, etc. The cops in the Sean Bell case fired- 50 bullets, killing this young man like he was an Al Qaeda operative or something. Included in the police report was that Mr. Bell or one of the other occupants had a gun, but there was no so- called gun found in the gun-riddled vehicle.

The odds of Mr. Bell making it back home and marrying his bride that week was pretty bleak because of some racist and paranoid policemen whom were probably raised to dislike black males. The officers involved waived their 'right to a jury, and the Judge acquitted the cop(s) involved. This is why, I use the term "systematic America" because this country operates systematically. For instance, we have the school system, penal system, judicial system, health system, et al., which are controlled by the white majority class at the expense of underclass minorities. The judge in this case didn't allow justice to run down like a mighty stream by prosecuting the policemen involved. It seems that Mr. Bell was just another statistic and trophy killing because the penal and judicial system operated by white males gave Mr. Bell's life little or no place value at all.

The staggering outcomes:

Historically, when it comes to the probability of black male, there are many cases of black men being accused and lynched for the demise of a white person; especially, in the Jim Crow South where crimes such as alleged rape has taken place. One particular case involved George Stinney, a 14-year-old black boy, executed in 1944 for allegedly killing two white girls ages 7&11 . What is so incredulous about this case is that 'Stinney's case intersects with some long-running disputes in the American's legal system about the death penalty and race *(Press, 2013)*. Stinney's siblings testified of his whereabouts saying that he was at home at the time of the so called murders. Notes from Stinney's confession and most other information deputies and prosecutors used to convict Stinney in a one-day trial have disappeared along with any transcript of the proceedings. A one-day trial for such a horrible crime is unacceptable. Killing a fourteen- year- old boy appeared to be second nature to these "blood thirsty" folks in the South. This case gives a glimpse of what it was like 'in the life a black male'. The probability of a black male leaving his home and being accused of raping a white woman in the South was about as imminent as 'the Second coming of Christ. There are critics that may say, "Well, that was the old South, can you find me something recent to support your claims?" As a matter of fact, there are recent and appalling cases. The two cases I'm about to share is disgusting, but proves that a black males chance of survival compare to his white counterpart is very slim.

Jason Smith' Story:

A 14-year-old Louisiana youth's death was ruled as an "accidental drowning," but his father is convinced he was murdered by the KKK. His organs disappeared. Some people think they were taken for transplants. However, the child had been dead for hours before his body was recovered from a lake. Could all of Jason Smith's organs have been stolen to hide the theft of his lungs, which could possibly have disproved the medical examiner's finding of "accidental drowning"? Jason's father alleges that one of Jason's murderers was the son of an FBI agent. He claims that police tried to kill him and another son on his way out of the Louisi-

THE UGLY SIDE OF AMERICA

ana town when he went to make final arrangements for his son. See one of the YouTube videos about Jason Smith at this link: http://www.youtube.com/watch?v=AAWgASicEk0 and embedded below. Jason's father buried his son on Father's Day.

Chavis Carter's Story:

Chavis Carter was arrested in Jonesboro, Arkansas. Police said Carter had drugs on him when arrested for missing a court date on drug charges. He was searched twice, double-locked in handcuffs, and locked inside a police car, but he allegedly pulled out a hidden gun and shot himself in the right temple although he was a left-handed young man. Carter's death was ruled a suicide, and The Cochran Firm frauds represent his mother (Neal, 2012). See the video embedded below at YouTube link
http://www.youtube.com/watch?v=naNwldJ78X4
I must say, "I thought this was just 'grapevine gossip when I found out about the Jason Smith story". When I typed in the link and watched the YouTube video of Jason smith's father, "It was a heart wrenching moment!" This stories were similar to the Emmitt Till case. These cases are real and prove we truly live in a society that doesn't value black males. The fact is that black males are more likely to be killed for their ethnicity more than any other ethnic group. Yes, a black male is also more likely to be killed by someone of his own race as well, but not based on skin color. This book is about "racially motivated" crimes against black males historically and existentially. After all, we live in a society where the first, biracial President presides, but real stories like Jason Smith and Chavis Carter, and others shouldn't be happening today. A biracial president in office is just anecdotal and doesn't "hate crime" proof black males. As a matter of fact, the election of Barack Hussein Obama has brought out the worse in America. We saw 'the beautiful side of America during the election and swearing in of President Barack Obama; however, we continue to experience 'the

ugly side of America when it comes to disparities, disproportionality, and inequality.

The fact is systematic America feels the black male is less than (<) white, Asian, and Hispanic counterparts. The order of equality is the issue and motivation for many of the social dilemmas that have affected black males. After all, historically and existentially, phobias about the black male have raised suspicions about racially motivated murders of black males, especially when there was an allegedly sexual component, in which a white woman was the victim. It's believed that a European phallus about the black male's sexual endowment exist amongst white females (see "fear and fantasy" Ch. 2), and white males have been the inferior ones falsely accusing black males of heinous crimes against white females; therefore, lynching, castrating, and burning countless black men over alleged murders and sexual assault offenses was common practice.

Murdering Mandingo:

Unfortunately, there seems to be a perpetual phobia towards black males; especially, when they fraternize with the forbidden fruit or national treasure (white women). I believe the 'Mandingo Mandate is still in effect today. We should examine some old ideology about black males to understand the historical and existential ideology. For instance, during the Apartheid in South Africa, black males were stigmatized and labeled by racist white colonialists. The two articles below shed light on the presuppositions mindset of colonist and the chronic criminalization of African black males.

According to Beiranvand & Liena, (2013):

In post apartheid South Africa, rape is a serious problem. Due to centuries of colonization, whites have a discriminatory attitude toward blacks and claim that the majority of rape victims are white women assaulted by black men. Similarly, white media disseminates the negative depiction of black men and gives cases of black peril broad coverage *(Beiranvand, 2013)*.

According to South and Felson, (1990):

When combined with increasing black identity and power, these contra cultural values lead blacks to strike out at the perceived source of their economic deprivation, viz., whites. Thus, both the frustrations of economic marginality and rising black politicization contribute to sexual attacks on white females *(South, 1990)*.

The articles touch on a misconception about black males. I talked about "fear and fantasy" in Chapter two, and how white women were forbidden from the black male slave, but white slave masters had no problem sexually intimidating and violating black female slaves. The fact is that both articles mention social conditions "Post Apartheid South Africa" and "frustrations of economic marginality and rising black politicization contribute to sexual attacks on white females" (South, 1990.) As far as Apartheid, I don't know if this was situational and retaliatory, but the perpetuation of this type of thinking has lead to stigmatization of many black males; it has led to them being falsely accused and murdered for raping white women. Unfortunately, there have been incredulous cases, in which some young black men were murdered for simply looking or talking to a white woman as in the Emit Till's story.

The fact is the "Mandingo mandate" has been implemented on young black males in the twenty- first century as well. There have been outlets like Hip hop, sports, and the entertainment industries for young black males to display their talents and enjoy the finer things in life; the American's pie has been laced with seduction and severe sentencing for many black men that enjoyed the forbidden fruit or national treasure, (the white female). There was one particular case involving Los Angeles Lakers' basketball star, Kobe Bryant. He was accused of allegedly raping a young, white female in a Denver, Colorado Hotel.

The report reads:

> On July 4, Sheriff Joe Hoy issued an *arrest warrant* for Bryant. Bryant flew from Los Angeles back to Eagle, Colorado to surrender to police. He was immediately released on $25,000 *bond* and news of the arrest became public two days after that. On July 18, the Eagle County District Attorney's office filed a formal charge against Bryant for sexual assault.

During the hearing, Mr. Bryant's attorney attacked the victims credibility. The investigation yielded that the victim wore underwear containing another man's semen and Caucasian pubic hair to her rape exam. The day of the alleged incident, Mr. Bryant's defense argued that the victim had another sexual encounter immediately after her encounter with basketball star Kobe Bryant. The victim told investigators that she grabbed dirty underwear by mistake from her laundry basket before the examination (Wikipedia, 2013).

The victim's name is withheld for safety reasons. However, the case allows one to see the lies and legal consequences that take place when affluent black males like Bryant find themselves accused of sexual interaction with a white female. The victim obviously had a fetish or fantasy for Kobe Bryant and consented to the sexual venture. In my honest opinion, I believe 'things got out of control and she couldn't handle Mr. Bryant's sexual dribble.

The evidence showed that this white female was lying and an opportunistic. She went looking for love in all of the wrong places and she found it; in the form of a well-built, black male that she couldn't handle in bed. I believe in this predominantly white region, the victim's parents and peers got involved and they were determined to make this successful black male pay for touching that hometown, lily-white girl by any means necessary. Thank God, Mr. Bryant was successful and had money to pay for legal representation to investigate the charges because many black males have been wrongfully accused, imprisoned, and lynched for touching or simply talking to a white women. It seems when a victim is white, black males are more likely to be accused and prosecuted for sexual allegations. The probability of a white male being accused, or even prosecuted for a sexual crime is extremely slim to none. The next case below is proof that white males are valued and vindicated even when direct evidence is smiling from ear to ear at the magistrates.

The report:

> Matthew Barnett (White male), then 18, was accused of raping then 14-year-old Daisy Coleman on January 7, 2012, at a party being held in the basement of his home. The Maryville High School football player -- who was a senior at the time – brought Coleman and her 13-year-old friend to his home, where Coleman says she was raped after she blacked out from drinking alcohol. Barnett, now 19, was initially charged with sexual assault and endangering the welfare of a child. But after just two months, the charges were dropped *(Green, 2013)*.

The fact that charges were dropped for Mr. Barnett is unbelievable. This clearly depicts inequality whereas the charges against Kobe Bryant were not dropped. This is where the order of equality (< >) comes to mind and racism is practiced in courtrooms. It doesn't matter if you're an affluent black male in America, you're still less than(<) your white counterparts. It seems that in these types of cases District Attorney's are more lenient on white males. I believe this is a systemic problem, but its foundation stems from Southern principles founded in Jim Crowism (see Michelle Alexander, The New Jim Crow, 2011-2102). The fact is young black males are being overwhelmingly targeted.

Alleged sexual harassment and assault accusations are common in middle and high school's as well; especially when the perpetrator is a black male, and the victim is a white female. The next case of Sam Mcnair (17) shows how far some will go unapologetically, to make a black male pay for tampering with a white female. The disparities between white males versus blacks accused of sexual crimes are just 'downright unacceptable.

The report reads:

> McNair, 17, was suspended on December 3 when a school hearing officer found he violated the Gwinnett County Public Schools' rules on sexual harassment. "Something so innocent can be perceived as something totally opposite," said McNair. A video of the hug, captured by a surveillance camera, shows McNair entered a room, placed his arms around the back and front of the teacher and tucked his head behind her neck. According to a discipline report, the teacher alleged McNair's cheeks and lips touched the back of her neck and cheek. McNair denied he kissed his teacher or sexually harassed her *(Chirico, 2013)*.

It's cases like these that make me very upset because I know how extreme educational policies such as "Zero tolerance" can be. Let me just say, "This case is unfortunate, but far too often, allegations are the lynch pin for derailing so many young black males like Mr. McNair. So many young black males acculturate into predominant white educational environments; however, when sexual allegations arise and the victim is a white female, the white educational legalists hide behind policy, criminalizing and penalizing young black boys more than their white male counterparts. Far too often, there is an aggressive mandate to charge the accused black males without a proper or measurable investigation. Normally, it's the word of the accused versus his accuser.

In addition, I believe many of the educational rules and policies that affect minorities were implemented as revenge for Civil Rights laws that catapulted minorities into mainstream America, and protected minorities such as Brown versus Topeka Board of Education (1954). Once integration was upheld and enforced by the Federal government; then came the covert racist rules, and policies that would impact minorities more than their white counterparts. This is why zero tolerance policies succeed in disproportionately affecting minority students. This may be due to "unconscious bias." *"Why else would we see, for the same first-time offense, blacks receiving harsh punishments far more often than whites?"* *(Klein, 2014)*.

Some of our educational policies are aggressive agendas to make our young boys and girls a statistic instead of a successful student and college hopeful. For instance, the 'prison industrial complex has been implemented on our school campuses in urban areas as well. There's a sinister scheme taking place in our public schools, especially in urban neighborhoods known as the school-to-prison pipeline. The trend is turning our adolescent students into criminals at alarming rates *(Brice, 2013)*. This is so true and the reason why we need more African American males in public school classes especially in urban areas. I believe African American father-figures are more important than gun wielding white authority figures on our school campuses, especially when it comes to African American children. I remember attending grade school and seeing quite a few African American male teachers. They were effective and did a wonderful job disciplining and imparting the lessons of the curriculum. For example, my sixth grade teacher, Mr. Tabb, an African American male gave me a severe dose of reality. One particular day, I was horse-playing around during gradu-ation rehearsal. Mr. Tab got angry and rushed towards me. He shoved me and gave me a mouth-full about "integrity" and "the real world." He said, "Bryant, you think this is some joke... you think in the real world (America)... you can horseplay and every-thing will be alright?" embarrassed with tears in my eyes, I re-sponded "No." he said, "You got that right... because your behind will be out on the streets without a job. Now... get to the Principals' office!" I was so embarrassed, but I knew in my heart that he cared about me and was doing what my own father would've done. Thanks to Mr. Tabb's shove and reality check, I started on the right track. Because of the chastisement of Mr. Tabb, I understand what he was trying to impart in me cautionary lessons about America.

The fact is that education and many other systems in America, were instituted by European whites males that had no intention of a black male being in a superior role, let alone becoming President of the United States. According to the Constitution's Fourteenth Amendment, the black male slave was considered unequal in intel-ligence compared to his white male counterpart. For instance, the Citizenship Clause provides a broad definition of citizenship, over-ruling the *Supreme Court's* decision in *Dred Scott v. Sandford* (1857), which had held that "Americans descended from African slaves could not be citizens of the United States (Wikipedia). Do you see the language involved? Those of African descendants were not valued, "Americans descended from African slaves could not be citizens of the United States." Why, because it goes back to "fear and fantasy" and order of inequality, and those mathematic symbols we were taught in public school (< >). Citizenship is about resources, privileges and honor; however, despite the blood, sweat, and tears of slavery, the black male was no more than 'chewing snuff and spit' under the white male's shoes. This is why laws and policies are so extreme towards minorities. The origin of something tells you a lot about its intent. *Historically, this is why the* "IQ" test was implemented to test intelligence. The black male was labeled unintelligent and not symmetrical (=) to their white male counterpart when it comes to intelligence. This is what systematic America is pretty much saying when black males end up in a Court of law, "You're guilty before proven innocent; you're unintelligent and you have no real place value in white America. Most of all, when you tamper with or are accused of fondling our forbidden fruit (white women), we, society, are going to ensure, we hang your black a** high... judicially!'

Affluenza: A white male's hall- pass

When it comes to the probability of a black male, it seems they're more likely to be prosecuted for similar crimes or less severe crimes than their white male counterparts. I believe systematic America has an honor and dishonor roll system; especially, when it comes to justice. The case below proves that something is definitely wrong with our judicial system and the order of equality is definitely applied. I believe some individuals go through the necessary channels and obtain a black robe, a mallet, to make sure white kids receive preferential treatment in court. The judge in the Ethan Couch case showed special treatment for the little Ricky Schroder (silver spoon type)-Ethan Couch.

The report reads:

> The defense was used in the case of 16-year old Ethan Couch, who got drunk, got behind the wheel, and proceeded to kill four people. He also paralyzed one of his friends, who was riding in the back of the truck. For some reason, Judge Jean Boyd bought the Affluenza defense, which is not recognized by the American Psychiatric Association, and gave Couch 10 years probation (Watkins, 2013).

Now, I've taken a enough courses to know that the Diagnostical Statistical Manual (DSM) is pretty much an important manual to psychologists in diagnosing conditions; however, "Affluenza" isn't included in the manual. The report says: "Affluenza is not recognized by the Psychiatric Association." The judge accepts some lame, immeasurable reason for Mr. Couch to avoid prison because she believed he doesn't belong behind bars. The judge approached this case with an "Order of equality" mentality that suggests Mr. Couch is not fit for prison because this young white male was perceived as being greater (>) than other individuals that commit similar or less crimes. We as society believe minorities who commit similar or lesser crimes do belong in prison as if incarceration is some type of normal habitat for minorities. So it's no big deal in sending a whole culture of black men to human warehouses by the groves while private corporations profit like Correction Corporation of America (CCA) . An African American teenager wouldn't have received preferential treatment in court. The fact is black males tend to be punished more than the their white male counterparts at an alarming rate. It seems that black and Latino males are perceived to be particularly a threat, dangerous and problematic. This results in judges singling them out for incarceration *(Tushar* Kansal, 2005).

Nevertheless, when we look at "the probability of a black male" and his existential plight; I must say, 'the future doesn't seem to be very promising. I believe the odds through: The flip of a coin, a roll of the dice, or a card picked from a deck espouses examples of probability. Hypothetically speaking, far too often, a coin with white supremacy on both sides of many outcomes; the societal dice given to the black male have been trick dice and contributed to them crapping out at the table of justice. Lastly, the cards dealt have come from a fix- deck ensuring they fold under socio-economical pressure. I believe America has already decided the fate of the black male and there's a monopoly on his freedom, function, and future role. I believe the devaluing of black males has been so traumatic that we've circumvented the frustration through self-hatred, unpatriotic sentiment, and criminal activity directed toward others and ourselves. This has also been an excuse for so many black men to defame their own culture and women, engage in domestic violence; placing a heavy load of single parenting on the black female. I believe America is either insane or inconsiderate of the outcomes of her treatment towards black males.

Action steps:

1. We need to protest against educational criminality on school campuses as well. There is disproportionality amongst African American males in regards to suspension and expulsion rates.

2. Volunteering our time on school campus and running for school board positions is key.

3. African American parents need to be aware and protest against the "school to prison pipe line" ploy on school campuses. The fact is African American and Latino males are more impacted than their white counter parts. See link: https://www.aclu.org/school-prison-pipeline

Nonetheless, the devaluing of black males has contributed to the breakage of the black family and many of the urban social ills. Historically and existentially, white power structures waged war on key individuals and organizations spearheaded by black men. Existentially, the prison industrial complex and pre-plotted social schemes have been major culprits in the devaluing and displacement of black males. This attack has set us back, in the black community, for years leaving so many black women fatherless and husbandless. Nevertheless, this brings me to the final chapter "*A black mother's load!*"

CHAPTER SIX

A Black Mother's Load!

"I finally understand
for a woman it ain't easy tryin to raise a man
You always was committed
A poor single mother on welfare, tell me how ya did it
There's no way I can pay you back
But the plan is to show you that I understand
You are appreciated"

-Tupac Shakur-

Momma's Babies, Daddy's Maybe:

There was a particular idiom, I often heard individuals spew out, called: "Momma's baby, Daddy's maybe." I didn't think much about its meaning at the time, but I believe the phrase was a cynical way of suggesting 'most women have carried the load of raising the children alone because of a deadbeat or absent father.' Unfortunately, it is a reality for some cultures, and in the African American community, single parenting statistics are staggering. According to government statistics, 72 percent of African-American children are born to unmarried mothers (Burton, 2010).

This is an unacceptable misfortune in the black community because some of the social ills that exist amongst black children is a result of single parent homes. One may counter my belief, and blame many of the woes of black males on other variables, but at the end the day, far too many black women are stuck with the responsibility of raising children alone.

I remember being about six years old, growing up, in Gardena, California. My dad was an ex Navy officer and with his GI bill he moved us into a decent middle-class neighborhood. However, one particular night, my parents got into a dispute over some infidelity on his part. My dad left, and I'd heard my sobbing mother from the other room. Later, an eviction notice followed the separation, and a U.S. Marshall escorted us out of the house. As my eleven siblings and I sat on the street curb, I looked over at my heartbroken mom with tears in her eyes. Hours went by until one of my aunties showed up in one of those old 1970 station wagons. We all packed in the station wagon like sardines and moved into my aunts' garage. Wow, it's hard to imagine a strong black woman and her eleven kids living in a garage. Months passed until my mom and dad reconciled: they bought another house in Los Angeles, CA. It was a three-bedroom fixer upper which was better than living in my aunt's overcrowded garage. Yes, my dad made a mistake, but I admired his courage and strength because he came back to his family and didn't place the heavy load of raising eleven children solely on my mom. Most men walk out and never return, but my dad listened to his conscience and came back to his family.

I shared this story because the pain of having to transition and live without my dad was traumatic. I believe my mom's heart was broken, not just because of my dad's infidelity; that's forgivable and healing can take place, but losing the first house we'd ever had was heart breaking. I believe this was the total sum of my mom's pain because she didn't want us to grow up without a father, but in a decent nuclear family. My mom sat there on that street curb determined to protect and provide for us...'by any means necessary. My mother's heart was broken by my dad's action, but come 'hell or high water' she wasn't about to abandon her babies. While sitting in despair on that curb and with tears in her eyes and pain in her heart, my mom reassured my siblings and I with these words, "Babies...everything is going to be all right." I believe this story is just one of many others that depict the heavy load women have to carry.

Moreover, I'm reminded of a particular story in the Holy Bible of a man that planted a seed, but abandoned his responsibility. This man put himself in a position to make a calculated choice, and because of his recklessness, he was the cause of a minority woman becoming a single parent in the process or what some call in the black community, a "baby momma". His name was Abram and her name was Hagar (Genesis 16:1-6). So after Abram had been living in Canaan ten years, Sarai his wife took her Egyptian slave Hagar and gave her to her husband to be his wife. He slept with Hagar, and she conceived. When she knew she was pregnant, she began to despise her mistress. Then Sarai mistreated Hagar; so Hagar fled (runaway slave) from her masters. NIV

First, I should point out that names in the Hebrew culture were important during this ancient setting because it was more about an individual's identity and destiny. The heavenly Father is the responsible party for the naming or renaming of an individual; for example, Abram (uncircumcised at the time) meant: exalted father, but his name was changed to Abraham-meaning: father of many, and Sarai was changed to Sarah- meaning: noble lady; Hagar (non Semitic), her name comes from "Ha-Agar," meaning this is the reward" and Ishmael means "God has hearkened."(Wikipedia). Isaac, which means God laughs was not born at the time, but he would eventually be the allotted son to carry on and enjoy the Abrahamic covenant. Hagar was the daughter of King Pharaoh of Egypt. When she saw the miracle which God performed for the sake of Sarah, to save her from the hands of the Egyptian king during Abraham's visit there, she said: "It is better to be a slave in Sarah's house than a princess in my own" (Mindel, 2014).

I should point out, that it was Sarai's choice for Abram to sleep with Hagar and give birth to a 'Son of the promise. In this type of paleo society, barrenness was thought to be a curse resulting from a sinful life. Secondly, there are circumstantial and consequential variables to consider. Hagar was a victim of circumstance in this story. She wasn't Jewish so she didn't receive a revelation about her situation until she was driven into exile or in lay-men terms: she was made into a single parent because of Sarah's paranoia at the time (Gen. 21:9). Hagar allowed a man to plant something on the inside of her that would serve as a "bitter sweet" investment. Thirdly, the story has a consequential component, al-lowing one to see 'Hagar's pain of raising a son alone. The reality is Abraham planted a selfish seed, but this doesn't suggest that Ishmael was a mistake in God's eyes. So many women reading this need to know that God understands, if you've made a mistake; just understand that the seed inside of you is useable and serves a pur-pose for God's glory.

I believe Hagar espoused great potential to be a "A good wife" and not just a love slave for an uncircumcised symbolic for (unre-generate) man at the time. I don't know what happened to Hagar after the prophecy in (Gen. 16:11), but she was exiled in (Gen. 21:14). My point is that God was with this single mom and made sure her son (Ishmael) was brought up to fulfill his destiny and re-ceive part of the Abrahamic blessing (Gen. 21:20-21).

Hagar's determination and strength was key for being success-ful in raising her son... alone. The fact is that Abraham put some-thing inside of Hagar that would be blessed by God. I believe so many women have to be careful about the man they date or marry because some have allowed a man to give them negative input or put something on the inside of them that's diametrically opposed to God's plan for their lives. After all, there are maxims that suggest, "When you lay down with dogs, you wake up with fleas." I be-lieve, this is the case for so many African American women that are raising children alone. Like Hagar, so many women are in a desert place in their lives without any help from a man; but to all of the Hagar's out there, you can wipe away the tears from your eyes because "God has hearkened your cry and He will alleviate your pain".

Nonetheless, Hagar received a "bitter sweet" prophecy from God about her son (Ishmael). God declared that because Ishmael was a result of Abraham, he would be a "blessed nation", but a "wild man" as well. This is important to point out because Ishmael being raised by a single mom in the wilderness came with consequences. The boy needed a father and the absence of such a key figure must have made Ishmael a recalcitrant type of individual. I believe during his adolescence, teenage and adult years he was aggressive, angry, and lacked a sense of authority. I believe that Ishmael observed the pain on his mom's face during his upbringing, and that the abandonment from his father, Abraham, caused him much trauma. It is understandable why Ishmael would turn out to be a "Wild man" according to the Bible (Gen. 16:12). Hagar went through a traumatic event of divorce and raising a son alone, especially, in a desert location which was hard labor. Ladies, can you imagine hot flashes in a desert place, with no man, no public assistance, just a divine revelation from a God...you just met through angelic intervention? Hagar's life was a testimony in and of itself. Nevertheless, this brings me to my point that so many black women are raising son's alone, especially those that live in low income housing where drugs and gangs claim the lives of so many young black males.

The pain of raising son's alone:

There are so many women raising children alone and I take my 'hat off' to such strong women, in particularly, black women because of the insurmountable odds they have to face. The fact is " No father in the home means that the children grow up without a male figure to look up to. This can be extremely damaging to a child even if they seem like they are fine" (Crossman, 2013). I agree with this author because God has given earthly fathers the ability to instill preparation, principles, and purpose, especially, when it comes to raising sons. I believe there is an identity crisis and personality disorder, not in the clinical, but cultural sense; in regards to so many African American males. American's culture used to be about fathers influencing their sons and leaving an inheritance of wealth and wisdom. However, if you ask many African American males about their relationship with their father, there's a disdain and passive disposition during the dialogue juxtapose to the relationship many black males have with their mothers. The conversation about their mom will normally light up a room and the song: "I'll always love my momma" by the Intruders can imaginatively be heard in the background. I believe a great love for mothers should be an important practice in the lives of our sons, but the disdain for fathers has resulted in social ills which have been overwhelming for single mothers.

Altruistically, it's black women who are attending parent-teacher meetings, basketball, football, and baseball games. Most of all, they're getting up early in the morning, heading to the prisons to console their sons and daughters. This is why, so many women can identify with the words of the rapper Tupac Shakur when he states, "I finally understand for a woman it ain't easy trying to raise a man" in the song Dear Momma. The song resonates with a lot of women struggling to raise children alone. According to one particular author, there seems to be 'misconceptions about single, black women raising sons alone.

The author says:

> Black women relinquished or excused themselves of the responsibility of raising their sons to become men because they have been brainwashed into believing that it is a man's job to do it. Thus, some women wait for a man that may or may not show up while they possess much of what it takes to raise a man. We aim to put an end to this phenomenon, as we want you to be clear that your son cannot be raised into a man without you (Bush, Mitchell and Faraji, p. 5, 2013).

I agree with the author. He is correct in their view of black women raising sons and the issues associated with doing it without a man. I believe the problem is much bigger than just raising sons and making sure they make it to college or corporate America. I believe it comes down to two words "praising" and "blazing" a trail for our children. The fact is that children look for praise and affirmation from their fathers more than from anyone. For instance, there's nothing like a son scoring a touchdown or scoring the winning shot for his team, and then looking over and seeing his father in the bleachers going buck wild... doing a little dance; saying, to other parents... "Yeah, that's my boy,... he gets it from his daddy...good job, Ray Ray!" A mother can do this as well, but a father praising his son quickens a child spirit causing him or her to hold their head up high, put on a cape, and feel they can conquer the world. I know this to be true when my son played football in his freshmen year of high school. He was happy when his mother attended his games, but he greatly desired my presence. He wanted to talk to me about the game, his plays, his successes and challenges. This was something he could not really do with his mom. It is clear that the presence of the father sparks an excitement that should be supported.

Secondly, I believe father's "Blazing" the trail for their son's is seemingly missing in so many African American homes as well. A father is the template that is set before children in regard to acceptance of authority and moral direction. Far too many children are expose to abuse instead of love in the home. A husband who kisses his wife and caresses her in front of the kids leaves a positive impression on the children. This helps boys to see how males should behave in a cordial manner towards the opposite sex. Unfortunately, so many African American women endure verbal and physical abuse. Some women face so much abuse that they have to check into a 'Shelter for Battered Women. Some women suffer the abuse because they feel it is better to have the husband in the home for the sake of the children, but this type of devotion can be detrimental as well . The fact is a male child that has witnessed domestic violence has a greater chance of perpetrating the cycle of violence he has witnessed. According to Dutton and Sonkin (2003), "Forty-five percent of male batterers witnessed partner aggressor in their families of origin is one of the most consistent predictors of male-perpetrated partner aggression" (Inititnate Violence, Contemporary Treatment Innovation, 2003). No woman should have to endure relationship terrorism; however, domestic abuse is a pervasive problem in the African American community as well.

Domestic Violence: "Who told Harpo to hit me?"

I believe most people in America are familiar with Ms. Oprah Winfrey's classic movie: The Color Purple, a novel by Alice Walker directed by Steven Spielberg. A Southern black woman sold into a life of servitude to her brutal husband, sharecropper Albert, Danny Glover. There character I would like to focus on is Ms. Winfrey's role as (Sophia), an African American, plus size, Southern woman that didn't take no guff from anybody. Mrs. Winfrey's role was quite polarizing in the film and just about every American household can testify to that. Nonetheless, here is the famed-line of Oprah's character.

Sophia:

> "All my life I had to fight. I had to fight my daddy. I had to fight my uncles. I had to fight my brothers. A girl child ain't safe in a family of men, but I ain't never thought I'd have to fight in my own house!" "I loves Harpo, God knows I do. But I'll kill him dead 'fo I let him beat me" (The Color Purple).

This was an encouraging scene in the movie because Sophia, was an encouragement for Celie, a fragile love slave to her abusive husband. Despite, the entertainment and casual mimicking of Oprah's famed-line on comedy shows, plays, and everyday settings in the African American community; the reality is, African American women suffer domestic abuse more than their white female counterparts. According to report: "Black women comprise 8% of the U.S. population, but in 2005 accounted for 22% of the intimate partner homicide victims and 29% of all female victims of intimate partner homicide" (University of Washington, 2014). Yes, so many women should arrive at a "no- guff" stance in their lives against an abusive spouse. The movie is made for the big screen, giving us a one-dimensional angle of domestic abuse. What goes on in the lives of so many women is actually appalling, and the story I'm about to share is most incredulous. An African American female victim, Lavon Morris, suffered a real case of domestic violence at the hands of her own unpredictable husband.

Lavon Morris:

> My husband who never physically abused, but in the end after I left him, he shot me four times; once in the head, thigh, buttocks and foot. My three children witnessed the shooting. Once I got us out of the house to safety, my husband shot himself once in the right temple; shattering his brain and dying 2 days later *(Moses, 2013)*.

First and foremost, this is an atrocious experience for any woman to endure. Mrs. Morris story is unique because of the non-detectors in her marriage. She said, "My husband who never physically abused, but in the end after I left him, he shot me four times." Domestic Violence is an issue as well that affects us all, whether it's at churches, schools, our neighborhoods or places of work. Domestic violence is a heavy, but unacceptable load for any women to endure. The question critics may ask, 'Why don't black men value their women? And how can black men expect systematic America to value them, when they don't value their own women? That's a legitimate assessment. However, there is a consensus of black men in the ecclesiastical community as well as organizations such as the Nation of Islam (NOI) that indeed value their women. These particular groups of men often make it their ministry to reach and teach misinformed and morally deformed young black males to honor their women and themselves.

When it comes to culture one has to take into consideration the sub-culture within a culture. For instance, some believe the prison industrial complex and hazardous Hip hop (gangster /commercialized rap) is the culprit for much of the defamation of black women. There's enough blame to go around especially, when it comes the statistic of 70% African American homes being headed by single parent females. The statistics on this issue should serve as a wakeup call for black males, but some conservatives insist on pointing an unfair finger at the Hip hop culture. I believe systematic America is 70% the blame because of the prison industrial complex and disparities that exist. There is also the contribution of joblessness and worthlessness. Some may ask, "What do you mean by joblessness and worthlessness? I've learned that the last stage or fate of an individual before he or she commits suicide is hopelessness. In such cases, like Levon Morris, perpetrators often experience some type of experience or event, which may include loss, traumatic childhood, or life threatening illness. Black men face many odds that may be uncommon in other cultures of men. The pressure can be overwhelming for some men, especially, if he feels his livelihood is threatening. It is harder for some black men to pick up the pieces after a loss like his white male counterpart because of the disparities that exist. When I refer to joblessness and worthlessness, I'm focusing on the opportunities, value, and treatment of the black males in systematic America. Unfortunately, Mrs. Levon Morris' husband couldn't handle the break up and the fact of being away from his children, so he reached a place of hopelessness and snapped. This is not justification for domestic abuse, but it is a personal psychological assessment as to why there are high statistics amongst African American women on issues such as domestic violence when certain variables are present.

The black male has an obligation to fight for his family and build on the shoulders of great men and women that have paved the way. Abandoning or abusing our women to the point that we don't even desire a black women during the pinnacle of one's success is nauseating. Instead of treating black women like queens and prospective housewives; so many black males resort to negative language to express their emotional instability on the inside because of an abusive father or abandonment at a pivotal time in their lives. The sad reality is, in the words of Ms. Morris, "In this society, we re-victimize victims all the time. Many children are witnessing abuse in the home and being abused as well and not receiving proper interventions to help them heal (Moses, 2013). So many women are raising children of their abuser, in particular sons. Sadly,, too many of these young men become successful men, according to white society standards, earning their way into industries and some are given a microphone to vent their negative childhood experiences. This is why defamation of black women has occurred, and the music industry has been infamous for the devaluing of black women as well. That's why it's easy for some men to call a woman a bad word or engage in domestic abuse because of exposure to such devaluing lyrics or abuse during their adolescence.

Who You Calling A Bitch?

I believe the disrespect directed towards black women is unacceptable and the entertainment industries have been favorable outlets for blaxploitation. Therefore, outlets for such defamation should be challenged to stop endorsing artists through negative media imagery and CD sales. If white women were being the objects of defamation, citizens would protest and demand the halting of any such media publication. Just like the "N" word, the "B" has become a term of endearment amongst the subculture in the African American community as well.

I remember hearing one a particular rap song called, "A Bitch is a Bitch" by Ice Cube AKA O'Shea Jackson. I respect Ice cube as a West Coast native and love most of his music that is urban, socioeconomical, and political, but this song stirred within me some negative emotions about some women; especially, those that may act inappropriate at times. I believe music can be a powerful tool or it can be a destructive outlet for miseducating at risk generations. Nonetheless, Hip hop is just a small problem to a historical deficiency in regard to the defamation of black women. For instance, white slave masters are the original "pimps" and "bitch callers" and it started the day that black women were brought over on slave ships, auctioned and raped by so many white men who took pleasure in sexually assaulting our women. This shouldn't serve as cause for maladaptive behavior towards black women by some misguided black males. No, this should serve as a decree to take inventory of our current plight as a culture and take responsibility for the domestic disrespect towards black women that has plagued our community. This a pivotal time for black women to look in the mirror, smile, and declare... that you are not a "B***h"; You're a queen, someone's mother, daughter, and sister. So the next time, you're shopping at a mall, grocery store, or walking your dog while wearing something sexy and some misinformed brother gets mad and calls you a "Bitch" because you don't have time for him, turn around and say to him... in a queen Latifah way, "Who you calling a bitch?" Once you have his undivided attention with piercing eyes, say to him, "If I'm a bitch, your momma is one." This is sure to get a man's attention because no man enjoys anybody talking bad about their momma.

Periodically, I'd come in contact with some black males in interracial relationships and the conversation about black women would conclude negatively. Some would share about a past experience they've had in a relationship with a black woman, and how things were not kosher; so they vowed to never date or marry another black woman. Several gentleman shared that they'd dated white women because "they're docile and programmable" and be-lieve most black women they've dated were "loud, lazy, and le-thal" to their success. This is a shame, how we've become a dis-colored and divergent generation of men as well. This behavior places a load on black women and makes it hard for them to find successfully descent black men. However, most successful black men are experiencing their share of hell... on earth; as result of wanting to date or marrying only white woman; just ask Tiger Woods, and others. We may not respect one another as men or tell each other... 'brother, I love. Nevertheless, let's at least value our women and help alleviate the heavy load many black women have to carry on their own.

Though this book is mainly about black males and racially motivated incidents, I included this chapter to focus on the impact that "the devaluing of the black males" has had on black women as well. Historically and existentially, the attack on a culture of men has ultimately devastated our women the most; leaving them fa-therless, husbandless, and sonless. After all, there have been many black women standing up for their husbands and have paid with their lives as well. For Instance, most people don't know about Black Women Who Were Lynched in America. However, accord-ing to Davis (2008) "Research has revealed there are over 150 documented cases of African American women lynched in America and four of them were known to have been pregnant" (Davis, 2009).

Action steps:

1. We need to restore African American marriages. We, as men, should take or remain in our rightful place and reduce the high single parent statistic.

2. Black women should institute an non- negotiable stand-ard and raise the bar in their lives as well.

3. We should protest television stations and demand more

positive images on television or stop supporting artist that don't contribute financially or in an acceptable manner to African American culture.

Nonetheless, if you're a black male reading this and you feel convicted about the contribution you've made towards the defamation of black women, I urge you to take a vow and change your current behavior. As men, we can't reverse past treatment towards us or our women, but we can dictate the future culturally, educationally, and socioeconomically by adding value to ourselves and our culture.

Epilogue

I remember attending a high school wrestling match where I had a chance to watch my son compete against another school. As I sat in the bleachers of a crowded gymnasium of predominantly Caucasian and Hispanic parents and students, I had this brief revelation about the black male's value in America. My son and his teammates gathered around a teammate, placing a hand on the young man's head chanting the words: "Titans on three... Titans on me... one, two, three- Titans,...aaahhh, rruuu!" Later, I ask my son, "Why did you guys place your hands on the head of your teammate(s) and chant those words?" My son gave an interesting response. He responded, "It's just something we do to send out our teammate(s) giving them encouragement and our blessing as a team...for victory over the competition."

I believe this is important for every black male to know because America has not positively gathered around the black male. Systematic America has adamantly and altruistically given her blessing to white, Asian's and alternatively Hispanic males, pronouncing blessings and victory over the competition (domestic and foreign). Unfortunately, instead of affirming and exhorting the black male with the words: "America on three, America on me, one, two, three blessings...aaahhh rruuu!" America, has grabbed the black male by the head, incarcerated, and unjustifiably murdered as many as possible. This has been an historical and existential reality for so many African American males.

Moreover, the trauma and wounds from such historical and existential ordeals are unforgettable. This is why I compare the attack on viable groups like the Black Panther Party (BPP) spearheaded by black males to sexual assault.. The only opportunities and organizations that existed in American history were destroyed by white perpetrators that were paranoid about black men who they assumed posed a threat. Certain groups of black men were just trying to build a brighter future for their own culture. When it comes to traumatic events such as rape, no one can put a timeline on a victim's recovery. There is no way disingenuous critics can place a deadline on the black male's recover of social terrorism that continue to exist in America.

I believe time is running out for America's opportunity to honor and treat the black male as an asset. The solution to "the devaluing of black males" is spiritual and societal. America is in an unregenerate state and needs a divine awakening. There's a hole in the soul of America that needs to be filled with racial equality. On the other hand, the black male has to take responsibility for his portion, illuminate self- hatred, and put our resources together like every other culture. Until these wonders take place, we cannot expect America to altruistically value us. I believe a "Purge" is underway to illuminate as many African American males as possible. There is a historical and existential pattern, in regards to racially motivated incidents. We have become a nonchalant nation, and as a black man I'm tired, tired of the devaluing of an entire culture of men: through stop and frisk, racial profiling, unarmed shootings, as well as mass incarceration!

Salient solutions:

The solution to the problem is not that complex, especially, if color coded America is willing to congruently value the black male.

- ➤ The hiring of more African American cops nationwide is a start. There's still disproportionality within law enforcement.
- ➤ The admittance of more African Americans in Ivy league colleges as well. There is still discrimination that takes place on college campuses, and most colleges are subliminally selective about the number of African American students they want admitted.
- ➤ Lastly, I believe stricter penalties and punishment should be handed down to cops for police brutality and unjustifiable homicides. There are just too many cases of unarmed shootings of black males in particular. Yes, I believe life terms and hefty restitutions should get the attention of those cops that feel they don't have to value the life of a civilian.

Book Club Discussion

1. As a society, how are we positioned to provide aggressive interventions to prevent the killing of so many black males?

2. Does society consider black Hip Hop artists a threat because of their access to wealth, white women, and their influence over the mind of white teens?

3. Mr. Bill O'Reilly stated: "If Trayvon Martin had been wearing a jacket like you or a tie,..Mr. West, I don't think George Zimmerman would've had any problem with Mr. Martin." Was this assessment accurate or disingenuous? Should we ban Hoodies and sagging pants and give fines ?

4. Have African American leaders blindly reinstated "the house Negro versus field Negro" mentality through conservatism versus liberalism? Are we too culturally disjointed to solve the current dilemmas of black America?

5. What does the future look like for American Americans based on the current disproportionality, incarceration, black on black crime and unjustifiable homicide rate?

6. Have successful black males compromised their commitment to the black culture due to their wealth and white notoriety?

7. How can we build self-sustaining Black communities where families can not only survive but thrive?

8. How can we encourage more marriage among Blacks, versus interracial marriages?

9. How can we use more extended family systems to help raise children since it takes a village to raise a child?

10. How can successful men help mentor young black boys to keep them on a positive path?

Bibliography

Alexander, M. (2010-2012). The new jim crow. Greene Street, New York: New New Press.

Anderson, C. (1994). Black labor, white wealth. In C. Anderson, Black labor, white wealth (p. 250). Bethesda, Maryland: PowerNomics Corporaion of America.

B., G. (2013 йил 13-Decmeber). Crowd funding campaign for documentary on The bloody massacre of blacks in Wilmington, NC. From The Balck Voice: http://www.yourblackworld.net/2013/12/black-news/crowd-funding-campaign-for-documentary-on-the-bl%CE%BFody-massacre-of-blacks-in-wilmington-nc/

Beiranvand, A. A. (2013). Black peril vs. white peril. A post colonial criticism on J. M. Coetzee's Disgrace, 59.

Berger, K. S. (2011). The developing person through the life span. New York, New York: Worth Publishers.

Botelho, G. (2014 йил 17-Feburary). Dunn convicted of attempted murder; hung jury on murder in 'loud music' trial. From CNN Jusitice: http://www.cnn.com/2014/02/16/justice/florida-loud-music-trial/

Breaking Brown. (2014, March 10). Retrieved from Minnesota Lawmaker: Street crime would decrease if NBA players disappeared: http://breakingbrown.com/2014/03/minnesota-lawmaker-street-crime-would-decrease-if-nba-players-disappeared/

Brice, B. (2013 йил 02-August). Dr. Byron Price Explains why schools are trying to get your child ready for prison. From Kulture Kritic: http://www.kulturekritic.com/2013/08/men/dr-byron-price-explains-why-schools-are-trying-to-get-your-child-ready-for-prison/

Burton, N. (2010 йил 09-November). 72 percent of african-american children born to unwed mothers. From The Root: http://www.theroot.com/articles/culture/2010/11/72_percent

_of_africanamerican_children_born_to_unwed_mothers.ht
ml

Byers, K. S. (2013 йил 20-November). Racial profiling: Shows unequal justice for blacks. From National Undergraduate Research Clearing House:

http://clearinghouse.missouriwestern.edu/manuscripts/403.php

Cadet, D. (2013 йил 18-10). Jordan Davis' shooter rants about killing 'thugs' so they 'may take the hint and change their behavior'. From HuffPost BlackVoices:

http://www.huffingtonpost.com/2013/10/18/jordan-davis-shooter-michael-dunn_n_4123805.html?ncid=edlinkusaolp 00000009

Chen, S. (2013 йил 21-10). CNN.com/us. From Growing hate groups blame Obama, economy:

http://www.cnn.com/2009/US/02/26/hate.groups.report/ind ex.html?_s=PM:US

Chirico, J. (2013 йил 17-December). CBS Atlanta. From student suspended for a year for hugging teacher:

http://www.cbsatlanta.com/story/24209980/student-suspended-for-a-year-for-hugging-teacher

Corey, G (2013), Theory and practice of counseling and psychotherapy (p. 534). Belmont, CA: Brooks/Cole.

Crossman, K. (2013 йил 26-December). Ladies: what we do to our kids when we raise them without their fathers. From Healthy Black Woman, Health Mind, Body & Soul:

http://www.healthyblackwoman.com/ladies-what-we-do-to-our-kids-when-we-raise-them-without-their-fathers/

Daniel J. Losen, J. a. (2010, September). Suspended Education. Retrieved from Southern Poverty Law Center SPLC: http://www.splcenter.org/get-informed/publications/suspended-education

Davis, H. V. (2009 йил 22-July). Recorded cases of black female lynching victims 1886-1957: More on black women who were lynched. From Henrietta Vinton Davis's Weblog: http://henriettavintondavis.wordpress.com/2009/07/22/reco rded/

DEFINITIONS OF: (2014 йил 06-Feburary). From Vocabulary.com: http://www.vocabulary.com/dictionary/discolour

Donald Dutton, & Daniel J. Sonkin . (2003). In initimate violence, Contemporary Treatment Innovation (pp. 260-261). Binghampton, NY: The Haworth Press, Inc.

Ehrenhaus, P. &. (2004). Race lynching and christian evangelicalism. Performances of Faith, 276-301.

Foster, T. A. (2011). Journal of the History of Sexuality. The sexual abuse of black Men, 447.

Friedman, A. (2013 йил 21-10). Times News Feed. From Trayvon Martin's Family on Zimmerman Apology: 'We Must Worship a Different God': http://newsfeed.time.com/2012/07/19/trayvon-martins-family-on-zimmerman-apology-we-must-worship-a-different-god/#ixzz216hJXVfn

Gaynor, G. K. (2014, March 31). White writer says black students lack 'impulse control' In classrooms. Retrieved from Centric: http://www.centrictv.com/whats-good/good-living/2014/03/31/white-writer-says-black-students-lack-impulse-control-in-classrooms.html

Geragos, M. (2013 йил 15-July). Trayvon was black. It matters. From The Daily Beast : http://www.thedailybeast.com/articles/2013/07/15/michael-jackson-lawyer-mark-geragos-on-race-and-trayvon-martin.html

Gower, R. (2005). Customs & manners of bible times (pp. 10-15). Chicago: Moody Publishers.

Green, T. (2013 йил 19-October). Who is matthewbBarnett? 7 Facts To Know About The Accused Maryville Rapist. From International Buisness Times: http://www.ibtimes.com/who-matthew-barnett-7-facts-know-about-accused-maryville-rapist-1433070

Harris, J. ". (2014 йил 11-Feburary). Tupac Shakur: The future of the black race lies within the young black male. From BOSS: http://www.brothersonsports.com/tupac-shakur-the-future-of-the-black-race-lies-within-the-young-black-male/

Huff Post BlackVoice. (2013 йил 07-July). From Juror B37 On Zimmerman Trial 'Sure' Voice On 911 Tape Was George, Not Trayvon Martin: http://www.huffingtonpost.com/2013/07/15/juror-b37-

zimmerman-trial-911-tape-george_n_3601501.html

Huff Post Media. (2013 йил 14-Septemeber). From Bill O'Reilly: Trayvon Martin died because he 'looked a certain way': http://www.huffingtonpost.com/2013/09/14/bill-oreilly-trayvon-martin_n_3926484.html

Jr., B. B. (2014 йил 26-Janurary). Kulture Kritic. From Study: Black fathers are the most involved dads in America: http://www.kulturekritic.com/2014/01/news/study-black-fathers-involved-dads-america/

Kimbrough, W. M. (2013, May 21). Why USC and not a black college, Dr. Dre? Retrieved from Los Angeles Times: http://articles.latimes.com/2013/may/21/opinion/la-oe-kimbrough-usc-dre-20130521

Klein, R. (2014 йил 03-Jan.). Zero-tolerance policies may make schools more unsafe, Report Finds. From Huff Post/ Black Voice: http://www.huffingtonpost.com/2014/01/03/school-zero-tolerance-policies_n_4538420.html?utm_hp_ref=black-voices&ir=Black%20Voices

Krout, K. (2013 йил 11-December). Divorce and fatherhood statistics. From SPARC Separated Parenting Access & Resource Center: http://www.deltabravo.net/cms/plugins/content/content.php?content.284

Lawson Bush V, Edward C. Bush. Kennon Mitchell, A. Majadi And Salim Faraji. (2013). The Plan: A guide for women raising African American boys from conception to college (p. 5). Chicago, IL: Third World Press.

Manus, P. M. (2010 йил 03-September). J Edgar Hoover: "The greatest threat to the internal security of the country". From FOR SOLIDARITY WITH THE OPPRESSED!: http://patrickmacmanus.wordpress.com/2010/09/03/j-edgar-hoover-%E2%80%9Cthe-greatest-threat-to-the-internal-security-of-the-country%E2%80%9D/

Massie, M. (2013 йил 16-July). The ugly truth about Trayvon Martin. From The Daily Rant: http://mychal-massie.com/premium/the-ugly-truth-about-trayvon-martin/

Mindel, N. (2014 йил 06-Jan.). Chabad. From Hagar:

http://www.chabad.org/library/article_cdo/aid/112053/jewish/Hagar.htm

Moses, N. M. (2013 йил 23-December). An advocate for abused women; Husband shot her four times, Including one shot to her head. From Healthy Black Women: http://www.healthyblackwoman.com/meet-lavon-morris-grant-an-advocate-for-abused-women-husband-shot-her-four-times-including-one-shot-to-her-head/

Muhammad, D. R. (2013, October 24). Black farmers say "Meet me half-way". Retrieved from Nation of Islam Ministry of Agriculture: http://www.noimoa.com/black-farmers-say-meet-me-half-way/

Neal, M. (2012 йил 03-September). Suicides, accidents and government murder cover-ups. From Mary Loves Justice: http://marylovesjustice.blogspot.com/2012/09/covering-up-black-mens-murders.html

Post, H. (2013 йил 13-11). These 32 people are spending their lives in prison for nonviolent crimes. From Blackvoice Huffington Post: http://www.huffingtonpost.com/2013/11/13/life-without-parole_n_4256789.html?ir=Black%20Voices&utm_hp_ref=black-voices

Press, A. (2013 йил 10-11). Huffington Post. From George Stinney: black teen executed In 1944, may get new trial: http://www.huffingtonpost.com/2013/11/10/george-stinney-black-teen-executed-new-trial_n_4250315.html?utm_hp_ref=black-voices&ir=Black%20Voices

Price, A. F. (2001). The white distortion, interweaving racism with relgion. In F. K. Price, Race Religion & Racism: Perverting the gospel to subjugate a people (p. 2). Los Angeles, CA: Faith One Publishing.

Racial Disparity. (2013 йил 22-Januarary). From the sentencing project: http://www.sentencingproject.org/template/page.cfm?id=122

Racial Profiling: Black NFL players get arrested 10 times as often as whites. (2013 йил 29-November). From YOUR BLACK

WORLD:
http://www.yourblackworld.net/2013/11/black-news/racial-profiling-black-nfl-players-get-arrested-10-times-as-often-as-whites/

Ralph, M. (2009). Social Text: Hip hop, 141 -146 Vol.27 Issues 3_100.

Richman, D. C. (2005). Al Capone's Revenge: AN Essay on the political economy of pretextual prosecution, 583.

Samuels, R. (2013 йил 3-October). Wikipedia. From: the murder and the movement. The story of the murder of Emmett Till: http://www.richsamuels.com/nbcmm/till/till.html

Savali, K. W. (2013 йил 26-July). Conservative black chick: Trayvon's mom 'manufacturing race war,' 'Didn't care about him'. From NEWS ONE:
http://newsone.com/2644059/crystal-wright-sybrina-fulton/

Scherker, A. (2013 йил 20-November). Huff Post . From teen thrown in violent new York prison for years without ever having been convicted:
http://www.huffingtonpost.com/2013/11/20/kalief-browder-rikers-teen-violent-new-york-prison_n_4302360.html?utm_hp_ref=email_share

Sean Bell. (2011 йил 01-December). From The New York Times: http://topics.nytimes.com/top/reference/timestopics/people/b/sean_bell/

Sharpton, R. A. (2013 йил 16-December). HuffPost Politics. From 'affluenza' and the miscarriage of justice:
http://www.huffingtonpost.com/rev-al-sharpton/affluenza-and-the-miscarriage-of-justice_b_4455301.html

South, S. J. (1990). The racial patterning of rape. Social Forces, 71-93.

Spivey, B. Y. (2013 йил 21-October). Stop Corporations from Profiting Off the Prison Business. From Black Blue Dog: http://www.blackbluedog.com/2013/10/news/stop-corporations-from-profiting-off-the-prison-business/

Spivey, Y. (2013 йил 13-December). The destruction of black wall street by american terrorists. From Your Black World: http://www.yourblackworld.net/2013/12/black-news/the-destruction-of-black-wall-street-by-american-terrorists/

This resolve was fueled by the results of two private investigators that the family hired to independently seek out answers. Harold Copus, the Atlanta private investigator that they hired, revealed that the head of the victim suffered some trauma which *co.* (2013 йил 13-10). From BlackBlueDog: http://www.blackbluedog.com/2013/10/news/private-investigator-says-police-story-about-kendrick-johnsons-death-is-flat-out-wrong/

Trayvon martin died Because he 'looked a certain way'. (2013 йил Friday-Septemeber). From The Raw Story: http://www.rawstory.com/rs/2013/09/13/oreilly-and-allen-west-agree-trayvon-martin-died-because-he-looked-a-certain-way/

Tushar Kansal. (2005). A review of the Literature. Racial disparity in sentencing, 17.

Tyner, J. A. (2006). Defend the Ghetto: Space and the urban politics of the black panther party. Annals of the Association of American Geographers, 108 & 114.

University of Washington. (2014 йил 06-Feburary). From Institute on Domestic Violence in the AfricanAmerican Community: http://www.idvaac.org/media/publications/FactSheet.IDVA AC_AAPCFV-Community%20Insights.pdf

Vernal, F. (2008). Slavery And Abolition. 'No such thing as a mulatto slave':, 27.

Waldrep, C. (August 01, 2008). National Policing: Lynching, and constitutional change. Journal of Southern History, 595-596.

Watkins, B. (2013 йил 14-December). Your Black World: From rich, white kids have affluenza, poor, black kids go to prison: http://www.yourblackworld.net/2013/12/uncategorized/dr-boyce-rich-white-kids-have-affluenza-poor-black-kids-go-to-prison/

Weiss, J. (2008 йил 27-March). Listen to and read the whole 'God damn America' sermon by the Rev. Jeremiah Wright. From The Dallas Morning News: http://religionblog.dallasnews.com/2008/03/listen-and-read-to-the-whole-g.html/

Welch, K. (2007). Journal of Contemporary Criminal Justice. Black criminal stereotypes and racial profiling.

Wikipedia. (2013 йил 25-October). William Lynch speech. CA, United States.

Wooten, S. (2013 йил 15-October). Political Blindspot: From man who shot 8-year-old child In the face gets bail reduced!: http://politicalblindspot.com/man-who-shot-8-year-old-child-in-the-face-gets-bail-reduced/

Young, T. (2011, December 22). Should Alan Hansen apologise for using the word 'coloured' on Match of the Day? Retrieved from The Telegraph: http://blogs.telegraph.co.uk/news/tobyyoung/100125547/should-alan-hansen-apologise-for-using-the-word-coloured-on-match-of-the-day/

www.ingramcontent.com/pod-product-compliance
Lightning Source LLC
Chambersburg PA
CBHW070204290526
45789CB00002B/912